Takaharu
+Yui Tezuka
NOSTALGIC
FUTURE
ERINNERTE
ZUKUNFT

jovis

Mit freundlicher Unterstützung von *Kindly supported by*

  箱根彫刻の森美術館
THE HAKONE OPEN-AIR MUSEUM

Medienpartner *Media Partner*

DETAIL

Takaharu +Yui Tezuka
NOSTALGIC FUTURE ERINNERTE ZUKUNFT

Paul Andreas & Peter Cachola Schmal (Hrsg. / Eds.)

Mit Beiträgen von *With contributions by*
Taro Igarashi, Joseph Grima & Paul Andreas

jovis

Imprint *Impressum*

This catalogue has been published to coincide with the exhibition "Tezuka Architects—Nostalgic Future" at the Deutsches Architekturmuseum (DAM), Frankfurt.

9 May – 28 June 2009

© 2009 by jovis Verlag GmbH, Deutsches Architekturmuseum DAM
Texts with kind permission of the authors. Pictures with kind permission of the photographers / holders of the picture rights. All rights reserved.

Edited by Paul Andreas and Peter Cachola Schmal

COPY EDITING Paul Andreas

DESIGN & SETTING Matthias Neuendorf (Tezuka Architects)

COVER DESIGN Gardeners, Frankfurt

TRANSLATION ENGLISH-GERMAN Sabine Bürger and Tim Beeby (Art Language), Petra and Jeremy Gaines (Gaines Translations)

TRANSLATION JAPANESE-GERMAN Wolfgang Höhn and Mariko Sakai

TRANSLATION JAPANESE-ENGLISH Thomas Daniell

PHOTOGRAPHS Katsuhisa Kida (Fototeca)
(except pp. 42—44, 47 © Tezuka Architects;
pp. 21—29 © Kai Kasugai)

PROOFREADING Philipp Sperrle, Markus Zehentbauer

PRINTING & BINDING GCC Grafisches Centrum Cuno, Calbe

Bibliographic information is published by Die Deutsche Bibliothek. Die Deutsche Bibliothek lists this publication in the Deutsche Nationalbibliografie; detailed bibliographic data are available on the Internet at http://dnb.ddb.de.

jovis Verlag GmbH
Kurfürstenstraße 15/16
10785 Berlin
www.jovis.de

ISBN 978-3-86859-021-0

Dieser Katalog erscheint anlässlich der Ausstellung "Tezuka Architects – Erinnerte Zukunft" im Deutschen Architekturmuseum (DAM), Frankfurt am Main.

9. Mai – 28. Juni 2009

© 2009 jovis Verlag, Deutsches Architekturmuseum DAM
Das Copyright für die Texte liegt bei den Autoren. Das Copyright für die Abbildungen liegt bei dem Fotografen / Inhabern der Bildrechte. Alle Rechte vorbehalten.

Herausgegeben von Paul Andreas und Peter Cachola Schmal

REDAKTION Paul Andreas

GESTALTUNG & SATZ Matthias Neuendorf (Tezuka Architects)

COVER DESIGN Gardeners, Frankfurt am Main

ÜBERSETZUNG ENGLISCH-DEUTSCH Sabine Bürger und Tim Beeby (Art Language), Petra und Jeremy Gaines (Gaines Translations)

ÜBERSETZUNG JAPANISCH-DEUTSCH Wolfgang Höhn und Mariko Sakai

ÜBERSETZUNG JAPANISCH-ENGLISCH Thomas Daniell

FOTOS Katsuhisa Kida (Fototeca)
(mit Ausnahme von S. 42–44, 47 © Tezuka Architects;
S. 21–29 © Kai Kasugai)

SCHLUSSLEKTORAT Philipp Sperrle, Markus Zehentbauer

DRUCK & BINDUNG GCC Grafisches Centrum Cuno, Calbe

Bibliografische Informationen werden von der Deutschen Bibliothek verzeichnet; detaillierte bibliografische Daten sind im Internet über http://dnb.ddb.de abrufbar.

jovis Verlag GmbH
Kurfürstenstraße 15/16
10785 Berlin
www.jovis.de

ISBN 978-3-86859-021-0

Contents *Inhaltsverzeichnis*

FOREWORD *VORWORT*
7   Peter Cachola Schmal & Paul Andreas

ESSAYS
10   "Straight Modern" or the Intensity of Architecture / Taro Igarashi
13   *„Straight Modern" oder die Intensität der Architektur*
16   An Architecture that Mimics People / Joseph Grima
18   *Architektur, die Menschen nachahmt*
21   Conversation with Takaharu and Yui Tezuka / Paul Andreas
26   *Gespräch mit Takaharu und Yui Tezuka*

PROJECTS *PROJEKTE*
32   Woods of Net
38   Fuji Kindergarten
48   Matsunoyama Natural Science Museum "Kyororo"
56   Eaves House
60   Cloister House
64   Atelier in Ushimado
72   GRV
76   Roof House
82   Toyota L&F Building
86   Wall-less House
90   Floating Roof House
96   Megaphone House
100   Engawa House

PLANS *PLÄNE*
105   Floor Plans, Sections, Elevations *Grundrisse, Schnitte, Ansichten*

SUPPLEMENT *ANHANG*
114   List of Works *Werkverzeichnis*
117   Biography *Biografie Tezuka Architects*
118   Contributors *Autoren*
119   Imprint Exhibition *Impressum Ausstellung*

Foreword

Peter Cachola Schmal / Paul Andreas

Three years ago, Deutsches Architekturmuseum DAM was gifted with an outsized model of the Natural Science Museum in Matsunoyama—a project designed by Tezuka Architects, Tokyo, which had become renowned far beyond the borders of Japan. During a trip to Japan's capital Mario Lorenz, a DAM collaborator came accross the model, which was destined to be scrapped following its exhibition in Tokyo's Gallery MA. It is made of sturdy corten steel and weighs over 300 kg and is 4.4 meters long. The architects agreed at short notice to gift it to DAM—and thus it was that an unusual exhibition project came to be.

At a second meeting with Takaharu Tezuka in January 2008, the idea of an exhibition swiftly gave birth to the idea of a workshop: admittedly, on the one hand we wished to avoid having to pay the horrendous transportation costs for presentation models and, on the other, everyone involved thought it would be worthwhile to link the overview of their oeuvre with a project that would involve dialog at many levels. We are very pleased that the DAM's ground floor will morph into an inter-university model building workshop for over a week, under the careful guidance of Takaharu and Yui Tezuka. We have architecture students from the Frankfurt University of Applied Sciences (Chair: Prof. Dunkelau), Wiesbaden University of Applied Sciences (Chair: Prof. Müller), Darmstadt Technical University (Chair: Prof. Eisele), and RWTH Aachen (Chair: Prof. Schmitz) to thank, as it is their models made on a scale of 1:50 from polystyrene but also wood as for the Hakone pavilion using traditional Japanese hand tools on a scale of 1:4 that provide an accurate account of how Tezuka Architects work.

The projects that we are showcasing in the "Tezuka Architects—Nostalgic Future" exhibition are perfect examples of the elementary strategies that architecture today can use to appear unconventional, without at the same time losing its earthing in everyday human life. Be it the many house projects with such seductive names as "Roof House" or "Wall-less House," cultural buildings such as the Matsunoyama Natural Science Museum or large edifices for small inhabitants, such as most recently the Fuji Kindergarten—the Tezukas show how using minimal but by no means minimalist means, an architecture can arise that interacts playfully with its users. Whether this lends architecture greater durability in an age of short-lived fads, which is what the architects hope, remains to be seen.

The DAM exhibition—which is also the first monographic show outside Japan (following their contributions to the 2002 Archilab and the 2004 Venice Biennal) —seeks to make a contribution here.

Peter Cachola Schmal
(Director of Deutsches Architekturmuseum)

Paul Andreas
(Curator of "Tezuka Architects—Nostalgic Future")

Vorwort

Peter Cachola Schmal / Paul Andreas

Vor drei Jahren erhielt das Deutsche Architekturmuseum als Schenkung ein überdimensioniertes Modell des Natural Science Museum in Matsunoyama – ein über Japan weit hinaus bekannt gewordenes Werk von Tezuka Architects, Tokio. Das Modell, das nach einer Ausstellung in der Gallery MA, Tokio, aus Platzgründen hätte verschrottet werden sollen – wegen seiner robusten Bauweise aus Corten-Stahl wiegt es über 300 kg und erstreckt sich auf einer Gesamtlänge von 4,40 Metern – entdeckte Mario Lorenz, ein Mitarbeiter des DAM, während eines Aufenthaltes in der japanischen Hauptstadt. Die Architekten erklärten sich spontan bereit, es dem DAM zu überlassen – und so nahm ein ungewöhnliches Ausstellungsprojekt seinen Ausgang. Bei einem weiteren Zusammentreffen mit Takaharu Tezuka im Januar 2008 wurde aus der Idee zu einer Ausstellung schnell die Idee zu einem Workshop geboren: Zugegeben, zum einen wollten wir die horrenden Transportkosten für Präsentationsmodelle einsparen – zum anderen fanden es alle Beteiligten aber auch lohnend, mit der Werkschau ein besonderes, in mehrerlei Hinsicht dialogisches Projekt zu verbinden: Wir freuen uns sehr, dass sich das Erdgeschoss des DAM unter Anleitung von Takaharu und Yui Tezuka über eine Woche lang in eine interuniversitäre Modellbauwerkstatt verwandeln konnte. Den Architekturstudenten der FH Frankfurt (Lehrstuhl Prof. Dunkelau), der FH Wiesbaden (Lehrstuhl Prof. Müller), der TU Darmstadt (Lehrstuhl Prof. Eisele) und der RWTH Aachen (Lehrstuhl Prof. Schmitz) danken wir; ihre Modelle im Maßstab 1:50 aus Polystyrol, aber auch das mit japanischem Handwerkszeug gefertigte Holzmodell des Hakone-Pavillons im Großmaßstab 1:4 geben ein treffendes Bild von der Arbeit und Herangehensweise des Büros Tezuka Architects.

Die Projekte, die wir in der Ausstellung „Tezuka Architects – Erinnerte Zukunft" zeigen, führen exemplarisch vor, mit welchen elementaren Strategien Architektur auch heute noch unkonventionell erscheinen kann, ohne dabei jedoch die Bodenhaftung im Alltag der Menschen zu verlieren. Egal ob es die vielen Hausprojekte sind, mit verführerischen Namen wie „Roof House" oder „Wall-less House", Kulturbauten wie das Matsunoyama Natural Science Museum oder große Bauten für kleine Bewohner wie zuletzt der Fuji Kindergarten – die Tezukas führen vor, wie sich mit minimalen, aber keineswegs minimalistischen Mitteln eine Architektur erzeugen lässt, die mit ihren Nutzern spielerisch interagiert. Ob das der Architektur in einer Zeit der Schnelllebigkeit wieder mehr Dauer verleiht, wie es die Architekten hoffen, muss sich erst noch weisen. Die Ausstellung im DAM – zugleich die erste monografische über die Architekten jenseits ihrer japanischen Heimat überhaupt (nach den Beiträgen zu den Archilab 2002 und 2004 Biennale Ausstellungen) – mag auch dazu einen Beitrag leisten.

Peter Cachola Schmal
(Direktor Deutsches Architekturmuseum)

Paul Andreas
(Kurator „Tezuka Architects – Erinnerte Zukunft")

Essays

"Straight Modern" or the Intensity of Architecture
„Straight Modern" oder die Intensität der Architektur

An Architecture that Mimics People
Architektur, die Menschen nachahmt

Conversation with Takaharu and Yui Tezuka
Gespräch mit Takaharu und Yui Tezuka

"Straight Modern" or the Intensity of Architecture

Taro Igarashi

I frequently receive invitations to weekend viewings of completed buildings by all sorts of architectural firms. Those sent by fax from Tezuka Architects are always something special. In addition to the address and the site plan, they contain something that is rare for architects nowadays: a sketch made with a thick pen. Even though the fax transmission means that the picture quality is not as good as it could be, the sketch provides an instant image of what is to be built: from the very outset, the Tezukas' buildings follow a clear concept. It seems to be important for them to state something using the power of the hand without relying solely on computer animations, as is so often the case. Takaharu Tezuka acquired the skill of producing powerful drawings in pencil when he was a student. And later, when he was working for Richard Rogers, he was held in high esteem because of his gift of producing perspective drawings off the cuff; in the Rogers studio he was also known as the "cartoonist."

POSITIONS IN JAPAN

Carried along on the wave of strong economic growth in the aftermath of WWII, the Metabolism group of architects designed their prestigious buildings. In the 1980s, architects born in the post-war era—such as Toyo Ito and Tadao Ando—took advantage of the favourable conditions of the "bubble economy" to complete major projects. At Atelier Bow-Wow (Yoshiharu Tsukamoto and Momoyo Kaijima), they were aware of the fact that they were making their debut at a time when there were no major projects; as such, over the past ten years they adopted a so-called "post-bubble" strategy.

In contrast, Takaharu Tezuka (born 1964) and his wife Yui (born 1969) are at pains to create something lasting: in their work they aim to avoid the impression of a relation to a specific time. As opposed to Atelier Bow-Wow, which uses the special characteristics of Tokyo as a strategic "weapon," Tezuka Architects endeavors to produce universal architecture based on Modernism, though local circumstances are very definitely integrated. This way they create spaces, which could be referred to as "straight modern."

However, what also distinguishes the Tezukas from other Japanese architects of their generation is their origin. Influenced by his father, who worked in the design office of the construction company Kajima Corporation, Takaharu Tezuka was surrounded by architecture books from a very early age. The family lived in a house the father had designed himself, and the young Takaharu is said to have played with his toy cars in his father's architecture models. When he was at primary school, he came across a special edition featuring buildings by Peter Chermayeff, which he repeatedly looked at until it was falling apart. What is also astonishing is that at that time he reproduced a plan of the Imperial Palace and is said to have even remembered the number of columns. Yui Tezuka's father also worked in an architectural studio (Daiichi Kobo Associates). Thus, the Tezukas are a family of architects of the finest pedigree.

As opposed to Takaharu Tezuka, who always wears blue shirts, red is Yui Tezuka's trademark. This is particularly noticeable at parties. Their two children wear yellow and green respectively, making the family's taste in fashion as obvious as that in buildings. Apart from this, the Tezukas are well known to a wide audience in Japan outside of the architectural scene—they have even appeared on popular TV shows. In comparison with other architects, they have also designed considerably more private houses.

A ROOM WITH A (NICE) VIEW

Based on buildings I have actually visited, I should now like to write about Tezuka Architects' work to date. The Wood Deck House (1999) marks the beginning of a series of buildings with a nice view. With its balconies, it opens out to the neighbouring woods. When the project was first published, the studio got more and more commissions for houses with a view of the sea or mountain landscapes; including, for example, the Megaphone House in Koshigoe (2000), which looks out over the Pacific (p. 96), and the Roof House (2001) (p. 76), from whose roof one can see the surrounding mountains.

The Roof House boasts not only tables and chairs, but also a kitchen and a shower so that it can be used for everyday activities. The individual rooms on the ground floor have skylights, to which wooden ladders lead. In this case, the client's wish to be able to enjoy his meals on the roof became architecture, though the roof is not the usual flat variety. Its slight incline and the missing boundaries define it as a roof in the classic sense.

The Megaphone House is a residential building with trapezoid footprint, perched on a cliff overlooking the sea. The main room, with its large 9 x 6-meter opening facing the sea became the living room. You don't have to be an expert in architecture to understand the message: this is a room in which you feel as if you are on a ship's deck. The ocean and the surroundings are reflected in the window and visitors can experience the play of the multifaceted refractions.

A SNAKE AND A RING

Tezuka Architects has nothing to do with an "aggressive avant-garde." In the case of the Temple to Catch the Forest (2007) in Yokohama, they did not overly emphasize that this was a hall for obsequies in a Buddhist temple. Even this religious project was developed informally on a larger scale using concepts that had proved their worth in building houses.

By way of contrast, the shape of the Matsunoyama Natural Science Museum "Kyororo" (2003) in Niigata (p. 48) seems complicated. The total length of the edifice is 120 meters; over 34 meters of the tip soar up as a viewing platform. The structure, which winds its way through the woods like a giant snake, is designed so that it follows a path through former rice terraces. Its design could be interpreted as the architects having lined up several copies of their Megaphone House next to each other like beads. The shape gives the impression of a legendary monster having suddenly appeared in the woods. Instead of scales, however, its entire body is covered with corten steel. The entrance, which is not protected by a roof in front, was cut into the exterior skin, so that visitors have the feeling of stepping into a giant snake's stomach. On the steel surface, the red rust creates texture patterns with an effect of depth, which in summer harmonizes with the green surroundings. It is almost as if "Kyororo" had been there for ages. However, if you visit the building in winter when there is deep snow on the ground, high walls of snow rear up on both sides of the approach road like raised layers of earth. The shape of the reptile is concealed then, as under the deep snow "Kyororo" has morphed into a tunnel. From large acrylic front windows one can observe the cut areas of snow—a fascinating image reminiscent of Romantic motifs. Here, too, you sense an atmosphere that surmounts time barriers.

Whereas "Kyororo" was a prize-winning competition project, the design for the Fuji Kindergarten (2007) in Tachikawa (p. 38) was the result of a recommendation by the well-known creative designer Kashiwa Sato. With this building, the giant elliptical shape around an interior courtyard is striking. The basic structure can be seen as a ring-shaped connection of several Roof Houses. In short, on its roof terrace not only a family, but more than 500 kindergarten children can play! And yet when you visit the kindergarten you are surprised by its small scale and the intimate impression the building makes.

On the inside, the number of pillars has been reduced to such an extreme that a single open room has almost been created. As there are no partitions to the outside either, the entire complex seems as transparent as a ring floating in the air. Although the formal features are clearly delineated, the architecture is not obtrusive. When I visited, I was fortunate to experience the general goings-on before lunch. The children came running into the courtyard from all directions and began playing. I was allowed to sit on the principal's chair and enjoyed the broad, panorama-like view, surrounded on all sides by children's voices. The patter of children running around on the roof also resounded from the ceiling. Having experienced this dynamic space using all five senses I was able to feel quite clearly how much the architecture is actually filled with life.

„Straight Modern" oder die Intensität der Architektur

Taro Igarashi

Von unterschiedlichsten Architekturbüros werden mir immer wieder Einladungen zur Wochenendbesichtigung fertig gebauter Häuser geschickt. Die Einladungen, die mir das Büro Tezuka Architects per Fax schickt, sind immer etwas Besonderes. Zusätzlich zu Adresse und Lageplan enthalten sie etwas, was heutzutage für Architekten selten ist: eine mit dickem Stift ausgeführte einfache Skizze. Auch wenn die Bildqualität wegen der Fax-Übertragung zu wünschen übrig lässt, zeigt diese Skizze doch auf den ersten Blick, was da gebaut werden soll: Die Bauten des Ehepaars Tezuka folgen von Anfang an einem ganz klaren Konzept.
Den beiden scheint es wichtig, etwas mit der Kraft der Hand mitzuteilen, ohne sich – wie sonst so oft – auf Computeranimationen zu stützen. Takaharu Tezuka hat sich die Fähigkeit, mit dem Bleistift kraftvolle Zeichnungen anzufertigen, während seines Studiums angeeignet. Und auch als er später im Büro von Richard Rogers arbeitete, wurde er wegen seiner Gabe geschätzt, Perspektivzeichnungen aus dem Stegreif anfertigen zu können: Im Büro Rogers nannte man ihn auch „Cartoonist".

POSITIONEN IN JAPAN

Getragen von der Welle des starken Wirtschaftswachstums schuf die Architektengruppe der Metabolisten in der Zeit nach dem Zweiten Weltkrieg ihre repräsentativen Bauwerke. Architekten wie Toyo Ito oder Tadao Ando, die in den 1940er Jahren geboren wurden, nutzten in den 1980er Jahren die günstigen Bedingungen der „Bubble Economy", um Großprojekte zu realisieren. Das Atelier Bow-Wow (Yoshiharu Tsukamoto und Momoyo Kaijima) war sich bewusst, dass es sein Debüt in einer Zeit ohne Großprojekte machte; man schlug im Laufe der letzten Dekade deshalb eine sogenannte „Post-Bubble"-Strategie ein.
Takaharu Tezuka (geb. 1964) und seine Frau Yui (geb. 1969) sind entgegen diesen Zeitströmungen bestrebt, etwas Beständiges zu schaffen: Den Eindruck einer Zeitbezogenheit wollen sie in ihrer Arbeit vermeiden. Im Gegensatz zum Atelier Bow-Wow, das die besonderen Eigenschaften von Tokio als eine strategische „Waffe" einsetzt, streben Tezuka Architects eine universale Architektur auf der Grundlage der Moderne an, wobei lokale Gegebenheiten durchaus einbezogen werden. So schaffen sie kraftvolle Räume, die man als „straight modern" bezeichnen könnte.
Was die Tezukas von anderen japanischen Architekten ihrer Generation unterscheidet, ist aber auch ihre Herkunft. Durch den Einfluss des Vaters, der im Konstruktionsbüro der Baufirma Kajima Corporation arbeitete, war Takaharu Tezuka von klein auf von Architekturbüchern umgeben. Die Familie wohnte in einem vom Vater selbst entworfenen Haus, und der kleine Takaharu soll mit seinen Spielzeugautos in den Architekturmodellen seines Vaters gespielt haben. In seiner Grundschulzeit fiel ihm ein Sonderheft mit Bauten von Peter Chermayeff in die Hände, das er sich immer wieder anschaute, bis es völlig zerlesen war. Erstaunlich

ist auch, dass er zu jener Zeit einen Plan des Kaiserpalasts nachzeichnete und dabei sogar die Zahl der Säulen im Gedächtnis behalten haben soll. Auch der Vater von Yui Tezuka arbeitete in einem Architekturbüro (Daiichi Kobo Associates). Die Tezukas sind also eine Architektenfamilie von echtem Schrot und Korn.

Im Gegensatz zu Takaharu Tezuka, der stets blaue Hemden trägt, ist Rot das Markenzeichen von Yui Tezuka. Das fällt auch bei Partys auf: Ihre beiden Kinder tragen jeweils Gelb und Grün, und so ist der Geschmack der Familie in der Mode genauso klar ausgeprägt wie bei ihren Bauten. Abgesehen davon ist das Ehepaar Tezuka in Japan auch einer breiteren Öffentlichkeit außerhalb der Architekturszene bekannt – selbst in populären Fernsehsendungen sind die Tezukas schon aufgetreten. Im Vergleich zu anderen Architekten ihrer Generation haben sie denn auch wesentlich mehr Privathäuser entworfen.

ZIMMER MIT (SCHÖNER) AUSSICHT

Ausgehend von den Bauten, die ich tatsächlich besuchten habe, möchte ich nun über das bisherige Werk von Tezuka Architects schreiben.

Das Wood Deck House (1999) eröffnet die Reihe der Häuser mit schöner Aussicht. Mit seinen Balkonen öffnet es sich zu einem benachbarten Wald. Nach der erstmaligen Veröffentlichung dieses Projekts gingen immer mehr Aufträge für Häuser mit Blick aufs Meer oder die Berglandschaft im Büro Tezuka ein. So etwa das Megaphone House in Koshigoe (2000) mit Ausblick auf den Pazifik (S. 96) oder das Roof House (2001), von dessen Dach aus man die umliegende Berglandschaft erblickt (S. 76).

Beim Roof House befinden sich auf dem Dach nicht nur Tisch und Stühle, sondern auch Küche und Dusche, sodass es sich für alle alltäglichen Aktivitäten nutzen lässt. Die einzelnen Zimmer im Erdgeschoss haben Dachfenster, zu denen Holzleitern hinaufführen. Der Wunsch des Bauherrn, auf dem Dach Mahlzeiten einnehmen zu können, ist hier Architektur geworden, wobei das Dach nicht das übliche Flachdach ist. Seine leichte Neigung und die fehlenden Begrenzungen identifizieren es als ein Dach im klassischen Sinne.

Das Megaphone House ist ein Wohnhaus mit trapezförmigem Grundriss, das auf einer Felsklippe über dem Meer ruht. Der Hauptraum mit seiner großen, zum Meer hin orientierten Öffnung von 9 x 6 Metern wurde zum Wohnzimmer gemacht. Man muss kein Fachmann für Architektur sein, um die Botschaft zu verstehen: Es ist ein Raum, in dem man sich so fühlt wie auf dem Deck eines Schiffes. Ozean und Landschaft spiegeln sich im Fenster, der Besucher kann dem Spiel der vielfältigen Lichtbrechungen beiwohnen.

SCHLANGE UND RING

Mit einer „offensiven Avantgarde" haben Tezuka Architects nichts im Sinn. Auch beim Temple to Catch the Forest (2007) in Yokohama haben sie nicht übermäßig darauf abgehoben, dass es sich um eine Halle für Totenfeiern in einem buddhistischen Tempel handelt. Selbst dieses sakrale Projekt wurde nach den im Hausbau erprobten Konzepten ungezwungen in größerem Maßstab entwickelt. Im Gegensatz dazu erscheint die Formgebung beim Matsunoyama Natural Science Museum „Kyororo" (2003) in Niigata kompliziert (S. 48). Die Gesamtlänge dieses Gebäudes beträgt 120 Meter;

über 34 Meter der Spitze strecken sich als Aussichtsturm in die Höhe. Der Bau, der sich wie eine Riesenschlange durch den Wald windet, ist so angelegt, dass er einem Feldweg zwischen vormaligen Reisterrassen folgt. Sein Entwurf kann so interpretiert werden, als hätten die Architekten mehrere Exemplare ihres Megaphone House wie bei einem Rosenkranz aneinander gereiht. Die Form erweckt den Eindruck, als wäre unvermutet ein legendäres Monster im Wald aufgetaucht. Statt mit Schuppen ist es jedoch am ganzen Körper mit Corten-Stahl bekleidet. Der Eingang, über dem keinerlei Vordach kragt, wurde in die Außenhaut eingeschnitten, sodass der Besucher das Gefühl bekommt, in den Bauch einer Riesenschlange einzutreten. Auf der Stahloberfläche bildet der rote Rost Strukturmuster mit Tiefenwirkung, die im Sommer mit der grünen Umgebung harmonieren. Fast könnte man meinen, „Kyororo" wäre schon seit Urzeiten da gewesen.

Besucht man den Bau hingegen im Winter bei tiefem Schnee, ragen auf beiden Seiten der Zufahrtsstraße Schneewände wie angehobene Erdschichten in die Höhe. Die Gestalt des Reptils bleibt dann verborgen, denn „Kyororo" hat sich unter der Last des Tiefschnees in einen Tunnel verwandelt. Aus großen Acrylfensterfronten kann man die angeschnittenen Schneeflächen betrachten – ein faszinierender Anblick, der an Bildmotive der Romantik erinnert. Auch hier spürt man eine Atmosphäre, die zeitliche Grenzen übersteigt.

Während es sich bei „Kyororo" um ein prämiertes Wettbewerbsprojekt handelte, entstand der Entwurf für den Fuji Kindergarten (2007) in Tachikawa auf Empfehlung des bekannten Creative Designers Kashiwa Sato (S. 38). Bei diesem Bau fällt die riesige elliptische Form um einen Innenhof auf. Die Grundstruktur lässt sich als eine ringförmige Verbindung mehrerer Roof Houses deuten. Kurz gesagt handelt es sich um einen Bau, auf dessen Dachterrasse nicht nur eine Familie, sondern mehr als 500 Kindergartenkinder spielen können! Und doch ist man, wenn man diesen Kindergarten besucht, überrascht vom intimen Eindruck des Gebäudes und seinem kleinen Maßstab.

Im Innenraum des Kindergartens ist die Zahl der Pfeiler so extrem reduziert, dass nahezu ein einziger offener Raum entstanden ist. Da es nach außen hin keine Trennwände gibt, erscheint die ganze Anlage so durchsichtig wie ein in der Luft schwebender Ring. Obwohl die formalen Merkmale deutlich ausgeprägt sind, drängt sich die Architektur nicht auf. Bei meinem Besuch hatte ich das Glück, den allgemeinen Trubel vor dem Mittagessen zu erleben. Von allen Seiten kamen die Kinder in den Innenhof gerannt und begannen zu spielen. Ich durfte auf dem Stuhl des Leiters Platz nehmen und genoss den sich weit öffnenden, panoramaartigen Ausblick, während mir von links und rechts Kinderstimmen um die Ohren flogen. Auch von der Decke her hallte das Getrappel der auf dem Dach umherlaufenden Kinder. Dank der alle fünf Sinne berührenden Erfahrung dieses dynamischen Raums konnte ich deutlich spüren, wie stark diese Architektur tatsächlich mit Leben erfüllt ist.

An Architecture that Mimics People
Joseph Grima

When setting up a practice, the first thing architects must design is their career. Depending on their skills, inclination and the depth of their pockets, they might decide to write a book or two, teach, or perhaps make paper architecture and draw. If they jump in the deep end and start practising, they will immediately face the biggest challenge of their career: the task of synthesizing their thinking and design philosophy into an architectural artifact that will attract broad attention, typically on a negligible budget, with a small staff, and with little experience.

In this scenario, architecture's most modest category—the single-family home—assumes gargantuan significance in the history of design. Small houses have revealed themselves to be a surprisingly accurate litmus test, not only of a designer's talents, but also of his aspirations. Early works are rarely the best, yet they typically synthesize the seed of an architect's thinking in its most pure and unadulterated form. In retrospect, it is clear that the Roof House by Takaharu and Yui Tezuka, built eight years ago now, was just such a case. This project, now a celebrated work of architecture—particularly in Japan—is distinguished by a single, dramatic alteration to the typical domestic layout: the living room, the hearth, the epicenter of family life, is displaced onto the roof—an inclined surface, open to the elements and to public view.

A radical act of subversion of the architectural norm, to be sure—but what does it tell us about Tezukas' design philosophy? A fundamental point here lies in the finality of this gesture. According to the architects, this is a reconfiguration of architecture to adapt to the family's habits, not vice versa: Takaharu and Yui Tezuka made it very clear that they did not see this as an opportunity to make a formal statement (indeed, at first glance it does not particularly stand out from the surrounding architecture), nor did they claim that they had invented a new domestic typology that improved the concept of dwelling as an architectural category.

It is in this sense that the Roof House, one of Tezukas' earliest projects, is a crystalline manifesto for the evolutionary objectives of their practice over the following decade. With one simple gesture on a low-budget dwelling—placing the living room on the roof—the Tezukas courageously defined their basic principles: theirs is an architecture driven by program, invention, and—inevitably—a questioning attitude towards the conventions of everyday life. Their architecture was not loud, but the ambition was evident in this very early project. Would they succeed, critical observers wondered, in upscaling these strategies into larger projects?

Considering the evolution of Japanese architecture over the past ten years, two distinct schools of practice are apparent. Already a decade ago, Japan easily occupied first place on the charts as the country with the highest standards and the greatest number of talented and ambitious small offices in the world. Delicacy, nuance, audacity, and spatial complexity abounded in architecture on every scale. Perhaps in response to the increasing density and fragmentation of the city, the deconstruction of domesticity (or at least the dramatization of its fundamental spatial components) became one of the prime preoccupations of a generation of younger architects such as Ryue

Nishizawa, Sou Fujimoto, and Junya Ishigami. A healthy percentage of their buildings use architecture to subvert and test the limits, rather than embrace Japanese society's domestic conventions: the bathroom might be a box in the garden with glass walls, as in Nishizawa's Moriyama House; a hyper-transparent dwelling might find privacy by standing above its surroundings on tall stilts, as in an unrealized proposal for a weekend home by Ishigami; or the living units might be stacked in an apparently haphazard, labyrinthine pile, as in some of Fujimoto's most recent residential projects.

In contrast to this, practices such as the Tezukas or Atelier Bow-Wow (Yoshiharu Tsukamoto and Momoyo Kaijima) opted for a strategy of "anti-astonishment." Mimicry is central to their design processes: while Atelier Bow-Wow look to urban microcosms such as the street, the neighbourhood, or informal architecture for inspiration, Tezukas' work looks to the identity, the interests, and the disposition of its inhabitants as the key forces in shaping its character. It is no surprise, therefore, that Tezukas' three best projects are centered around three very different programs and operate on very different scales.

The submarine-grade construction of the Natural Science Museum is, in engineering terms, the direct expression of the extreme nature of the environment it inhabits, but its architectural strategy is simple: given the location, little more need be done than expose the visitor directly to the power of nature, and this the museum does to stunning effect.

Fuji Kindergarten, on the other hand, builds on the concept of the Roof House, transforming the building's roof into a key programmatic area for the children's entertainment and education; beyond that, it is remarkable in that it is one of the few educational buildings that does not negate but celebrates the collective nature of education.

Instead of attempting to isolate classes into silent boxes, children are continuously exposed to the sights and sounds of others playing, rehearsing, and running in the central playground. This might easily be mistaken for an unintended byproduct of a formal choice (the kindergarten's iconic circular form) but, in fact, the reverse is true: the choice of the playful, slightly imperfect loop configuration with trees sprouting from the top is the direct expression of a programmatic decision, as well as a metaphor for society's embrace of a new generation.

In this sense, the course the Tezukas have plotted is very close to the one they originally charted: a quiet appreciation of architecture's potential, an uncommon experiential break from the loud gestures of formalism. Their best buildings are often the quietest, the simplest, those that are most closely driven by their programs. Their architecture is a comfortable fit for everyday life.

Architektur, die Menschen nachahmt

Joseph Grima

Wenn ein Architekt ein Büro eröffnet, muss er erst einmal seine Karriere planen. Je nach seinen Fähigkeiten, Neigungen und finanziellen Möglichkeiten entscheidet er sich vielleicht, das ein oder andere Buch zu schreiben, zu unterrichten oder zeichnenderweise Architektur auf dem Papier zu entwerfen. Wenn junge Architekten ins kalte Wasser springen und sofort in die Praxis einsteigen, sehen sie sich unmittelbar der größten Herausforderung ihrer Karriere gegenüber: Sie haben die Aufgabe, ihre Vorstellungen und ihre Designphilosophie in einem architektonischen Artefakt zu synthetisieren, das möglichst viel Aufmerksamkeit auf sich ziehen soll, und dies mit einem kleinen Budget, wenigen Mitarbeitern und kaum Erfahrung.

In diesem Szenario erhält die bescheidenste Kategorie innerhalb der architektonischen Entwurfsgeschichte, die des Einfamilienhauses, eine außerordentliche Bedeutung. Kleine Häuser sind der erstaunlich aussagekräftige Nachweis nicht nur der Begabung eines Architekten, sondern auch seiner Bestrebungen. Frühe Entwürfe sind selten die besten, doch bieten sie eine Synthese der Keimzellen der jeweiligen konstruktiven Vorstellungswelt in ihrer reinsten und unverfälschtesten Form. In der Rückschau betrachtet, ist das Roof House von Takaharu und Yui Tezuka, das bereits vor acht Jahren gebaut wurde, sicherlich ein solcher Fall. Dieser – vor allem in Japan – inzwischen zu Berühmtheit gelangte architektonische Entwurf unterscheidet sich durch eine einzige, jedoch drastische Veränderung der typischen räumlichen Anordnung eines Privathauses: Der Wohnraum, gewissermaßen die Feuerstelle und damit das Herz des Familienlebens, wurde auf das Dach verlagert – eine geneigte Fläche, die sich den natürlichen Elementen und zur Außenwelt hin öffnet. Sicherlich eine radikale Subversion der architektonischen Norm – aber was verrät sie uns über die Gestaltungsphilosophie der Tezukas? Ein wesentlicher Punkt liegt in der Entschiedenheit der Geste. Den Architekten zufolge handelt es sich um eine architektonische Neukonfiguration, die sich familiären Lebensgewohnheiten fügt und nicht umgekehrt. Es ging weder darum, eine formale Aussage zu machen (auf den ersten Blick scheint sich das Roof House tatsächlich auch nicht auf besondere Weise von der umgebenden Architektur zu unterscheiden). Noch beanspruchen die Architekten für sich, eine neue Typologie des Wohnbaus erfunden zu haben, die das Konzept des Wohnhauses als architektonische Kategorie verbessern würde.

In diesem Sinne stellt das Roof House als eines der frühesten Projekte ein kristallklares Manifest für die Entwicklungsziele ihrer Arbeit im nachfolgenden Jahrzehnt dar. Für ein Projekt mit geringem Budget und mittels einer schlichten Geste – die Verlagerung des Wohnraums auf das Dach – definierten die Tezukas grundlegende Prinzipien: Ihre Architektur ist programmatisch und erfinderisch, und sie zeichnet sich dadurch aus, dass die Konventionen des Alltagslebens unweigerlich hinterfragt werden. Auch wenn es kein lauter Entwurf war, lag die Intention, die sich hinter diesem Projekt verbarg, auf der Hand. Aber würden sie es schaffen, so fragten sich kritische Beobachter, diese Strategie auf größere Projekte zu übertragen?

Betrachtet man die Entwicklung der japanischen Architektur in den letzten zehn Jahren, sind es insbesondere zwei verschiedene Schulen, die sich abzeichnen. Schon vor einem Jahrzehnt konnte Japan, als Land mit den höchsten Standards und den meisten kleinen Büros mit ambitionierten und talentierten Architektenteams, den ersten Platz der Bestenliste geradezu selbstverständlich für sich beanspruchen. Die Architektur hatte Raffinesse, Zwischentöne, Mut und räumliche Komplexität zu bieten, ganz gleich, ob es sich um kleine oder große Projekte handelte. Die Dekonstruktion der Häuslichkeit (oder zumindest die Dramatisierung ihrer grundlegenden räumlichen Komponenten) wurde, vielleicht als Reaktion auf die zunehmende Verdichtung und Fragmentierung der Stadt, zur Hauptbeschäftigung einer ganzen Generation junger Architekten wie Ryue Nishizawa, Sou Fujimoto, Junya Ishigami. Bei vielen ihrer Gebäude werden die häuslichen Konventionen der japanischen Gesellschaft nicht aufgenommen, sondern durch die Architektur untergraben und infrage gestellt: So kann etwa das Bad eine Box mit Glaswänden im Garten sein, wie bei Nishizawas Moriyama House; eine völlig transparente Behausung erhebt sich auf Stelzen über ihre Umgebung und erhält dadurch Intimität, wie bei einem nicht realisierten Entwurf für ein Wochenendhaus von Ishigami; oder es sind scheinbar willkürlich und labyrinthisch übereinander gestapelte Wohneinheiten wie bei den jüngsten Wohnhausprojekten von Fujimoto.

Im Gegensatz dazu bevorzugten Büros wie Tezuka Architects oder Atelier Bow-Wow (Yoshiharu Tsukamoto und Momoyo Kaijima) die Strategie des „Anti-Spektakulären". Im Mittelpunkt ihres Gestaltungsansatzes steht die Nachahmung. Während man im Atelier Bow-Wow auf der Suche nach Inspiration auf den urbanen Mikrokosmos der Straße, der Nachbarschaft oder informellere Architektur blickt, sind bei den Entwürfen der Tezukas die Identität, die Interessen und das Wesen der Bewohner der Hauptantrieb für die Gestaltung. Es überrascht daher nicht, dass den drei besten Projekten von Tezuka eine jeweils andere Idee zugrunde liegt und sie in völlig unterschiedlichen Dimensionen funktionieren.

Der U-Boot-artige Bau des Natural Science Museum ist, konstruktionstechnisch gesehen, der unmittelbare Ausdruck der extremen Bedingungen der das Gebäude umgebenden Natur, die architektonische Strategie ist denkbar einfach: In Anbetracht des Ortes musste nicht viel mehr getan werden, als den Besucher die Kraft der Natur gewahr werden zu lassen, was mit diesem Museumsbau auf verblüffende Weise gelungen ist.

Auf dem Konzept des Roof House beruht der Fuji Kindergarten, der das Dach zum Mittelpunkt des Spiel- und Lernbereichs für die Kinder macht; abgesehen davon ist es bemerkenswert, dass es eines der wenigen Gebäude für den pädagogischen Gebrauch ist, bei dem das kollektive Wesen der Bildung nicht negiert, sondern gefeiert wird. Anstatt Klassen in ruhigen, voneinander separierten Räumen zu isolieren, werden die Kinder konstant dem Anblick und den Geräuschen anderer spielender, lernender oder umher rennender Kinder ausgesetzt. Dies könnte leicht als ungeplanter Nebeneffekt einer formalen Entscheidung (die bezeichnende Kreisform des Kindergartens) aufgefasst werden, aber das Gegenteil ist der Fall: Der spielerische, leicht unvollkommene kreisförmige Grundriss des Gebäudes mit Bäumen, die aus ihm heraus wachsen, ist der unmittelbare Ausdruck einer programmatischen

Entscheidung als auch eine Metapher für das Willkommenheißen einer neuen Generation durch die Gesellschaft.

Insofern ist die Richtung, die die Tezukas mit ihren Entwürfen eingeschlagen haben, ihrem ursprünglichen Gestaltungsansatz sehr eng verbunden geblieben: eine stille Anerkennung der Möglichkeiten, die Architektur eröffnet, ein ungewöhnlicher experimenteller Bruch mit den lauten Gesten des Formalismus. Ihre besten Gebäude sind häufig die leisesten, die schlichtesten, jene, die ihrem Konzept am treuesten bleiben. Ihre Architektur ist eine komfortable Passform für den Alltag.

Conversation with
TAKAHARU + YUI
TEZUKA

Paul Andreas

When I came to your office this morning, I was surprised to see you passing by with your two children in your yellow 2CV car. That's a very rare experience in Tokyo where everybody is commuting by trains. Tell me, what is your life like in Tokyo?

We try to make the living quality as good as possible in Tokyo. We try to create the kind of life we had in London—our office and house are situated quite close to each other, just five minutes by car. We enjoyed living in London very much. Even if the salary Takaharu got at Richard Rogers was low …

… at that time (at the beginning 1990s) his office wasn't doing well because of the recession.

… but in London there are so many parks and green spaces, and we could enjoy cycling along the Thames. There were so many things we could do without money. (laughs)

You are not living in central Tokyo, but in the less dense outskirts. "Little London" in Tokyo?

Not really. I can say that I never liked Tokyo, and I never wanted to come back here although this is where I was born. Tokyo is a very strange place. We architects can do whatever we want. So everybody tries to show what he is capable of—that is what we don't like about Tokyo.

So when you came back from London in the mid-1990s and opened up your office here, what did you want to change?

When we came back, I wasn't happy at all with what was published in Japanese magazines. We didn't want to do the kind of gymnastics that were shown there. We wanted to go back to the basics of architecture, which was no longer fashionable. We do something very calm and modest, but still we try to show a new vision.

The title of our exhibition will be "Nostalgic Future." Could you tell me what it is you want to recall with this ambiguous title?

When people were becoming rich, architects tried to get air-conditioned controlled space. At the same time, we tried to do futuristic designs for hotels—that used to be a kind of status. Nowadays, it is different: we have excellent technology. We can realize the nostalgia of our own memories and recreate the human experience we shared in the past. We can even enhance it and make it better than it actually was! So if you look at the Fuji Kindergarten, the structure and all kinds of details are extremely advanced, but you don't perceive the technology. It is a very simple building that seems to be timeless, which is quite important, because architects design structures for the next fifty or hundred years, or for centuries.

Architecture with such a long lifetime—hasn't that thinking been overcome, especially in Japan where houses used to be demolished every twenty to thirty years?

Most Japanese architects say that Japan is a country of temporariness, and that Ise Shrine has been rebuilt almost every twenty years, and that this would be an essential part of our culture. But it is not true because I know that my grandfather's house in Southern Japan is there for more than 120 years and our family has been living in the same plot for more than twenty-six generations! It was after WWII that people were taught that Japanese culture is temporary, but it was mainly for economical reasons and in order to change our existence into Western lifestyle, denying Japanese culture.

Is there any familiarity between your grandfather's house and what you are doing?

The openness of the space is a constant quality of Japanese architecture, which we like. At the same time my grandfather's house has excellent details. It has a beautiful corner in the guestroom, which can be opened completely, even the amado (rain door) isn't kept at the corner of the space. It was designed when my family used to conduct trade with the East-Indian company, but that kind of invention is still valid these days. There are so many things that have never lost their qualities.

Modern Japanese houses don't care about the climate of Japan very much. They are just imported and are built for the profit of the manufacturer, but not really for the convenience of the people. We try to recreate a kind of architecture that fits the Japanese climate, like the old, traditional Japanese house did.

When you were starting your office, you began with individual house projects—was that a credo or a necessity?

No, it was normal: we didn't have any other projects. It was my friend's house we started with.

But we enjoyed it, because to think about the house is the beginning of architecture. What we have learned from houses can be applied to any kind of architecture. We still believe our experience can be attached even to airport buildings. – Did you know that I was trained as an airport architect in Richard Rogers' partnership? The first plan I drew was 1:5000 scale for Terminal 5 at Heathrow.

But your architecture looks quite different from what we are accustomed to from Richard Rogers.

Yes, but his influence is very strong. The project we like most is his mother's house in Wimbledon, a very simple gate-shaped house. There are two sides totally open so you don't perceive a boundary between inside and outside and they have a beautiful garden. When we were there, his mother "Dada" said to us: "Did you know that I have taught Richard Rogers? I made him famous." At that time she was about 80 years old, wearing a green dress and looking herself like an art object; her existence was somehow competing with the Calder sculptures in her house.

When we saw his mother's house we found out that the concept of the architecture has to be felt inside without any words. That is the most important thing for architecture. In contrast, the concept for architecture in Japan is too difficult for common people who use the architecture to understand. And architects think that lay people belong to a different world, which they never have to consider.

Architecture needs to be understood by people. Therefore, the concept must be very simple.

When we designed the Roof House we strongly felt that there is a strong relationship between the lifestyle of the owner and architecture itself. When the client's family moved in, we felt that the Roof House started to live; it started to breathe (laughs). The relationship is so close—we felt that people are the last piece of the puzzle for doing architecture.

How did you succeed with that last piece? Have you had long discussions with the clients? How was the communication?

The Takahashi family invited us to their former house, which wasn't modern at all—nothing was particularly beautiful, but every piece, every corner of the kitchen had a thought. Then they took us to the upper floor to show us where they had lunch usually. You can imagine, how surprised we were when we climbed up the roof! Then the wife said that she would like to have a kind of tower on the roof so that they could watch the sea. Actually there was no sea to watch because the mountains there are quite high, but still she was keen on it! When designing the house, we finally picked up this essence of their lifestyle. We wanted them to get to know what they have, maybe even who they are.

What was their reaction when you presented your design to them?

They understood our idea immediately. But even more important: they think that they created the concept of the house by themselves! That kind of misunderstanding is very important. Actually, we planned it, we designed it, but the point is that every member of the family thinks "I am the one"!

Sounds to me like a subversive strategy. How would you describe your role as an architect under these conditions?

I wouldn't say we must have one role, we should have a diversity of roles as architects. However, we can say what we want: we want our architecture to exist beyond centuries. To achieve this, there is only one way: architecture has to get the fondness of the people who use it. With our projects we discover the nostalgia a family or the local people might have.

The important thing is that architects have to design an event that happens in the building. The windows, the height, and the scale of the volumes—all of these aspects of form and space are connected to this event.

We even design for slightest differences of inclination. Once in an exhibition, we showed hundreds of models of the Roof House—you could realize that the inclination of the roof was slightly different and also the height was gradually modified. We believe that such a slight gesture has a deep impact on the lifestyle.

Apart from the clients—when doing your projects don't you feel the necessity to develop some primordial ideas in your designs apart from the local conditions?

We are not trying to make a manifesto. Once you make a manifesto, the manifesto tries to drive your design. Many critics ask us: "What kind of style would you go for next?" They are expecting us to change, but we don't want to change. I think we should bring the change from the environment around us. When you get a new assignment, there are so many things to learn. We try to be a machine responding to requests—if our mechanism tends to hear the request we get a good answer; if we improve ourselves at the same time, then we get even better answers. We are changing gradually.

Even if you try to respond to the client and his requests, your projects can be easily identified as a Tezuka project. How do you achieve this?

Well, whenever we get a client we try to bring them into our house, the Saw Roof House. We listen to their requests but we also try to show them what kind of lifestyle we want. When we make the first scheme, we don't want them to get the contract—that's quite opposite from most of the architects. When they don't like it, we stop and say good-bye. Once we design something we enter a lifelong relationship. With most of the clients we have a very good relationship.—It is a kind of club. Only a few months ago there was a gathering in the Megaphone House, because clients know each other quite well, they even have a network. They talk to each other …

—without us. (laughs)

… they never call us, but somehow they get together quite well. They share their ideas.

Todoroki Office,
Tokyo, 16 February 2009

Gespräch mit
TAKAHARU + YUI
TEZUKA

Paul Andreas

Als ich heute morgen auf dem Weg in Ihr Büro war, sah ich Sie mit Ihren beiden Kindern in einem gelben 2CV vorbeifahren. Das hat mich etwas überrascht, denn in Tokio sieht man das selten, da jedermann mit dem Zug pendelt. Erzählen Sie mir, wie ist Ihr Leben in Tokio so?

Wir versuchen, uns so einzurichten, dass wir eine möglichst hohe Lebensqualität haben. In gewisser Weise versuchen wir ein ähnliches Leben wie in London zu führen – unser Büro und Haus liegen ziemlich nahe beieinander, lediglich fünf Minuten mit dem Auto. Das Leben in London hat uns sehr gefallen. Auch wenn das Gehalt, das Takaharu bei Richard Rogers bekam, nicht gerade hoch war …

… zu jener Zeit (Anfang der 1990er Jahre) lief das Büro wegen der Rezession nicht so gut.

… aber in London gibt es so viele Parks, und es ist so grün, es hat viel Spaß gemacht, an der Themse entlang zu radeln – es gab so viele Dinge, die wir ohne Geld tun konnten. (lacht)

Sie leben nicht im Zentrum von Tokio, sondern in einem weniger dicht bebauten Außenbezirk – „Little London" in Tokio?

Nicht wirklich. Ich mochte Tokio noch nie, wenn ich das so sagen darf. Und ich wollte auch nie wieder nach Tokio zurückkommen, obwohl ich hier geboren bin. Tokio ist ein seltsamer Ort. Als Architekten können wir hier machen, was wir wollen. Also versucht auch jeder zu zeigen, wozu er in der Lage ist – das mögen wir an Tokio nicht.

Als Sie Mitte der 1990er Jahre aus London zurückkamen und hier Ihr eigenes Büro eröffneten, was wollten Sie da verändern?

Als wir zurückkamen, gefiel uns gar nicht, was in den japanischen Zeitschriften so veröffentlicht wurde. Wir wollten diese Verrenkungen nicht mitmachen, wie sie da vorgeführt wurden, sondern lieber zu den Grundlagen der Architektur zurückkehren, etwas, das schon lange kein Thema mehr war. Unsere Arbeit ist leise und bescheiden, aber wir wollen dennoch eine neue Vision zeigen.

Der Titel unserer Ausstellung wird „Erinnerte Zukunft" sein – können Sie erklären, an was Sie mit diesem mehrdeutigen Titel erinnern wollen?

Als die Leute reich wurden, versuchten wir als Architekten, klimatisierte Räume zu schaffen. Zugleich versuchten wir, futuristische Entwürfe für Hotels zu machen – das war ein gewisser Status. Heute ist das anders: Wir haben eine ausgezeichnete Technologie. Wir können die Nostalgie unserer eigenen, schönen Erinnerungen realisieren und die menschliche Erfahrung wiederbeleben, die wir in der Vergangenheit teilten. Wir können sie sogar noch optimieren und besser machen, als sie eigentlich war! Sehen Sie sich den Fuji Kindergarten an: Die Konstruktion und alle Details sind sehr innovativ, aber man nimmt die Technologie nicht wahr. Es ist ein sehr einfaches Gebäude, das zeitlos zu sein scheint – Zeitlosigkeit ist wichtig, da wir als Architekten Architektur für die nächsten 50 oder 100 Jahre oder gar Jahrhunderte entwerfen.

Architektur mit einer solch langen Lebensdauer – ist das nicht eine Vorstellung, die überholt ist, insbesondere in Japan, wo Häuser gewöhnlich nach 20 oder 30 Jahren abgerissen werden?

Die meisten japanischen Architekten sagen, dass Japan ein Land der Kurzlebigkeit ist. Der Ise-Schrein werde alle 20 Jahre wieder neu aufgebaut, und dies sei ein grundlegender Aspekt der japanischen Kultur. Aber das stimmt nicht, denn ich weiß, dass das Haus meines Großvaters in Südjapan seit mehr als 120 Jahren steht und meine Familie seit mehr als 26 Generationen auf demselben Grundstück lebt! Nach dem Zweiten Weltkrieg vermittelte man den Leuten, dass die japanische Kultur einen temporären Charakter habe, aber das geschah hauptsächlich aus wirtschaftlichen Gründen und um unsere Lebensbedingungen unter Verleugnung der japanischen Kultur einem westlichen Lebensstil anzupassen.

Gibt es Bezüge zwischen dem Haus Ihres Großvaters und dem, was Sie heute tun?

Die Offenheit des Raumes ist ein konstantes Merkmal der japanischen Architektur, und das mögen wir. Zugleich zeichnet sich das Haus meines Großvaters durch großartige Details aus. Im Gästezimmer gibt es eine sehr schöne Ecke, die vollständig geöffnet werden kann, noch nicht einmal der Amado (=Regentür) bleibt dort stehen. Die Ecke wurde entworfen, als meine Familie mit der Ostindien-Kompanie Handel betrieb,

aber diese Art von Erfindungen haben heute noch immer ihren Wert – es gibt so viele Dinge, die nie ihre Qualitäten eingebüßt haben.

Moderne japanische Häuser sind nicht auf das Klima in Japan ausgerichtet. Sie wurden lediglich importiert und für den Profit des Herstellers gebaut, aber nicht wirklich für die Annehmlichkeit der Menschen, die in ihnen wohnen. Wir versuchen, eine Form von Architektur wiederzubeleben, die dem japanischen Klima entspricht, wie es bei den traditionellen alten japanischen Häusern der Fall ist.

Als Sie Ihr Büro eröffneten, begannen Sie mit einzelnen Häuserprojekten – war das Ihr Credo oder eher Notwendigkeit?

Nein, es war, wie es immer ist: Wir hatten keine anderen Projekte. Wir haben mit dem Haus von Freunden angefangen.

Aber es hat uns Spaß gemacht! Über ein Haus nachzudenken ist sozusagen der Anfang der Architektur. Was wir von den Häusern gelernt haben, kann auf jede Form von Architektur übertragen werden. Wir sind der Meinung, dass unsere Erfahrungen sogar auf Flughafengebäude angewendet werden können. – Wussten Sie eigentlich, dass ich als Flughafenarchitekt ausgebildet wurde im Büro von Richard Rogers? Der erste Plan, den ich gezeichnet habe, hatte einen Maßstab von 1:5000 für den Terminal 5 in Heathrow.

Aber Ihre Architektur ist ganz anders als das, was wir von Richard Rogers kennen.

Ja, aber sein Einfluss ist sehr stark. Das Projekt von ihm, das wir am meisten mögen, ist das Haus seiner Mutter in Wimbledon, ein sehr einfaches Haus in der Form eines Tores. Auf zwei Seiten ist es völlig offen, sodass man keine Grenze zwischen Innen und Außen wahrnimmt, und es hat einen sehr schönen Garten. Als wir dort waren, sagte „Dada", seine Mutter, zu uns: „Wussten Sie, dass ich Richard Rogers gelehrt habe, ich habe ihn berühmt gemacht." Damals war sie 80 Jahre alt, sie trug ein grünes Kleid und sah selbst wie ein Kunstobjekt aus – in ihrer Erscheinung konkurrierte sie gewissermaßen mit den Skulpturen von Calder in ihrem Haus.

Als wir das Haus der Mutter sahen, erkannten wir, dass das architektonische Konzept sich im Inneren ohne Worte eröffnet. Das ist das Wichtigste in der Architektur. In Japan hingegen können normale Leute, die die Architektur benutzen, das architektonische Konzept nicht verstehen, da es zu schwierig ist. Und Architekten glauben, sie müssen sich nicht mit der anderen Vorstellungswelt der Leute auseinandersetzen.

Architektur muss von den Leuten verstanden werden. Das Konzept muss einfach sein.

Als wir das Roof House entwarfen, waren wir überzeugt davon, dass es eine starke Beziehung zwischen dem Lebensstil des Besitzers und der Architektur gibt. Als die Familie des Auftraggebers in das Roof House einzog, hatten wir den Eindruck, dass das Haus nun zu leben beginnt – es fing irgendwie an zu atmen. (lacht) Die Beziehung ist so eng – wir finden, dass die Menschen das letzte fehlende Puzzlestück sind, wenn man Architektur macht.

Wie ist Ihnen das gelungen mit diesem Puzzlestück – mussten Sie lange mit den Auftraggebern diskutieren? Wie war die Kommunikation?

Die Familie Takahashi lud uns in ihr früheres Haus ein, das ganz und gar nicht modern war – nichts war wirklich schön, aber jedes Stück, jede Ecke der Küche war durchdacht. Dann zeigten sie uns das Obergeschoss, wo sie normalerweise zu Mittag aßen. Sie können sich vorstellen, wie überrascht wir waren, als wir das Dach hinaufkletterten! Die Ehefrau erklärte uns, dass sie gerne einen Turm auf dem Dach hätte, damit sie aufs Meer schauen könnten. Sie hat das einfach so empfunden – eigentlich gab es dort kein Meer zu sehen, da die Berge ziemlich hoch sind, aber sie wollte es trotzdem gerne! Als wir das Haus entwarfen, widmeten wir uns insbesondere diesem Aspekt ihres Lebensstils. Wir wollten, dass sie erkennen, was sie haben, vielleicht sogar, wer sie sind.

Wie war ihre Reaktion, als Sie den Entwurf präsentiert haben?

Sie haben unsere Idee sofort verstanden. Aber noch wichtiger: Sie glauben, dass das Konzept des Hauses von ihnen selbst entwickelt wurde! Diese Art des Missverständnisses ist sehr wichtig. Eigentlich haben wir es geplant, gestaltet, aber tatsächlich denkt jedes Familienmitglied: „Ich war derjenige!"

Klingt nach einer ziemlich subversiven Strategie – wie würden Sie Ihre Rolle als Architekten unter diesen Bedingungen beschreiben?

Ich finde nicht, dass wir Architekten nur eine Rolle haben können, es sollte eine Vielfalt an architektonischen Lösungen geben. Aber wir können sagen, was wir wollen: Wir wollen eine Architektur, die zeitlos ist. Um dies zu erreichen, gibt es nur einen Weg: Die Architektur muss die Zuneigung jener Menschen gewinnen, die sie benutzen. Mit unseren Projekten nähern wir uns der Nostalgie, die Familien oder die Menschen vor Ort vielleicht empfinden.

Wichtig ist, dass wir als Architekten ein Ereignis kreieren müssen, das sich im Gebäude abspielt. Die Fenster, die Höhe und der Maßstab des Bauvolumens – all diese Aspekte von Form und Raum sind mit diesem Ereignis verbunden.

Bei unserer Entwurfsarbeit bedenken wir sogar die kleinsten Unterschiede der Neigungswinkel. Wir haben in einer Ausstellung einmal hundert Modelle des Roof House gezeigt – man merkte, wie die Neigung des Daches etwas variierte, und auch die Höhe wurde leicht verändert. Wir sind davon überzeugt, dass eine so schlichte Geste trotzdem einen großen Einfluss auf den Lebensstil hat.

Abgesehen von den Auftraggebern – wenn Sie an Ihren Projekten arbeiten, empfinden Sie unabhängig von den örtlichen Gegebenheiten nicht die Notwendigkeit, einige wirklich grundsätzliche Gestaltungsansätze zu entwickeln?

Wir wollen kein Manifest aufstellen. Wenn man einmal ein Manifest hat, bestimmt das Manifest die Gestaltung. Viele Kritiker fragen uns: „Welchem Stil werden Sie als nächstes folgen?" Sie erwarten eine Veränderung von uns – aber wir wollen uns nicht verändern. Ich finde, die Veränderung muss aus unserer Umgebung kommen. Wenn man einen neuen Auftrag bekommt, gibt es so viele Dinge zu lernen. Wir versuchen, wie eine Maschine auf Wünsche zu reagieren – wenn der Mechanismus die Wünsche erkennt, bekommen wir eine gute Antwort; wenn wir uns zugleich verbessern, erhalten wir noch bessere Antworten. Wir verändern uns allmählich.

Auch wenn Sie versuchen, den Wünschen Ihres Auftraggebers zu entsprechen, können Ihre Projekte leicht als Tezuka-Projekt identifiziert werden – wie gelingt Ihnen das?

Immer wenn wir einen Auftraggeber haben, versuchen wir, ihn in unser Haus zu bringen, in das Saw Roof House. Wir hören uns seine Wünsche an, aber wir versuchen, ihm auch zu zeigen, welchen Lebensstil wir haben. Wenn wir die erste Zeichnung machen, müssen Sie noch keinen Vertrag mit uns abschließen – das ist bei den meisten Architekten ganz anders. Wenn Sie den Entwurf nicht mögen, hören wir auf und verabschieden uns. – Es ist wie ein Klub. Vor wenigen Monaten erst gab es eine Versammlung im Megaphone House, da die Auftraggeber sich untereinander recht gut kennen, sie haben sogar ein Netzwerk. Sie reden miteinander …

– ohne uns. (lacht)

… sie rufen uns nie an, aber kommen irgendwie zusammen. Sie teilen eine Idee!

Todoroki Office,
Tokio, 16. Februar 2009

Projects *Projekte*

Woods of Net

Fuji Kindergarten

Matsunoyama Natural Science Museum "Kyororo"

Eaves House

Cloister House

Atelier in Ushimado

GRV

Roof House

Toyota L&F Building

Wall-less House

Floating Roof House

Megaphone House

Engawa House

Woods of Net

This is a pavilion dedicated to a single artwork, which was created by Toshiko Horiuchi Macadam for the Hakone Open-air Museum. The artwork is a net structure with which children can interact by climbing, jumping, and rolling on it. The work had to be protected from rain and ultraviolet light, but we felt the net would look much better in an outside location but within a protective construction.

The structure consists entirely of wood. No steel reinforcements are used except for the base. It is a reference to the seventeenth century Kiyomizu temple in Kyoto, which was constructed by using a traditional joint technique no longer in use today.

The structure totals 320 cubic meters of wood comprising 580 individual pieces of wood. Each piece has been designed as a very complex shape in order to carry loads from different directions and of differing kinds, and at the same time allowing water to drain from the wood as quickly as possible to avoid warping. The entire structure was designed on a computer, the data was fed into a CNC trimming machine capable of carving out shapes that are precise to 0.1 millimeters. The pieces were lifted by a crane, yet are joined utilizing the very same techniques carpenters used 400 years ago.

In dem Pavillon für das Hakone-Freilichtmuseum ist nur ein einziges Kunstwerk ausgestellt. Es handelt sich dabei um ein riesiges Netzobjekt der Künstlerin Toshiko Horiuchi Macadam, in dem Kinder klettern, springen und umherrollen können. Es ging darum, das Netz vor Regen und UV-Strahlung zu schützen, aber wir entschieden uns dennoch für einen Standort im Freien, abgeschirmt unter einer Schutzvorrichtung.

Die Konstruktion besteht vollständig aus Holz. Mit Ausnahme des Fundaments kam keinerlei Stahlverstärkung zum Einsatz. Als Vorbild für die Konstruktion diente der Kiyomizu-Tempel in Kyoto, ein Bauwerk aus dem 17. Jahrhundert, das traditionelle japanische Holzverbindungen nutzt.

Die 320 Kubikmeter Holz umfassende Konstruktion besteht aus insgesamt 580 einzelnen Holzelementen. Jedes Einzelteil wurde in seiner komplexen Form individuell entworfen, um die verschiedenen, aus unterschiedlichen Richtungen auftretenden Kräfte aufnehmen zu können sowie ein sofortiges Abfließen des Regenwassers zu gewährleisten und somit einem Verziehen des Holzgerüsts vorzubeugen. Nachdem die komplette Struktur am Computer modelliert war, wurden die Daten in einer CNC-Fräse eingespeist, die Formen auf 0,1 mm genau zurechtschneiden kann. Die Teile wurden dann mithilfe eines 25-Tonnen-Krans an Ort und Stelle positioniert, die Verbindungen jedoch von Zimmerern genau so verkeilt, wie es vor 400 Jahren üblich war.

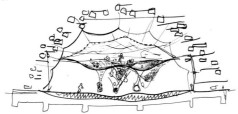

Fuji Kindergarten

A large oval building with an outer circumference of about 183 meters, and an inner circumference of about 108 meters. The architecture's structure is breached by three existing Zelkova trees, and provides a kindergarten for 560 children.

All of the architectural spaces are of a scale suitable for a child. It is a single-storey building, with the ceiling heights restricted to 2.1 meters. Hence, there is an extremely close relationship between the level of the floor and the level of the roof.

The childcare rooms contain—and are also subtly divided from each other by—furniture of a size and weight that a child can carry. The furniture can sometimes also become big building blocks.

The entire garden can be viewed from wherever you are. Our theme here is the "end of an era." This is a treasure house of the "joy" that we have abandoned in modern times. Modern conveniences have deprived children of sensation. What we want to teach through this building is "common sense." We want the children raised here to grow into people who do not exclude anything or anyone. Even though decades may pass, this kindergarten will still be full of the smiles of children running around energetically.

Ein großer ovaler Ring mit einem äußeren Umfang von rund 183 Metern und einem inneren Umfang von rund 108 Metern, wobei der Verlauf des Ovals von drei japanischen Ulmen unterbrochen wird: Dies ist ein Kindergarten für 560 Kinder.

Die gesamte Architektur ist den Größenverhältnissen eines Kindes angepasst. Bei einer Deckenhöhe von nicht mehr als 2,10 Metern liegen in dem einstöckigen Gebäude Fußboden- und Dachebene extrem nah beieinander.

Die Räume zur Kinderbetreuung sind mit Möbelstücken von einer Größe und einem Gewicht eingerichtet, wie sie von einem Kind getragen werden können. Zudem werden Möbel raffiniert als Trennelemente zwischen den einzelnen Räumen eingesetzt, und auch als große Bauklötze lassen sie sich benutzen.

Auf dem Grundstück ist der gesamte Garten von jedem beliebigen Standort aus zu überblicken. Unser Thema lautet hier: „Das Ende eines Zeitalters". Der Komfort des modernen Lebensstils beraubt die Kinder der natürlichen Sinneseindrücke. Dieses Haus hütet einen heutzutage seltenen Schatz – die Freude. Was wir mit diesem Gebäude vermitteln möchten, ist „gesunder Menschenverstand": Wir wünschen uns, dass die Kinder, die hier aufgezogen werden, zu Menschen heranwachsen, die nichts und niemanden ausgrenzen. Auch in Jahrzehnten wird in diesem Kindergarten noch immer das Lachen von rennenden und tobenden Kindern erklingen.

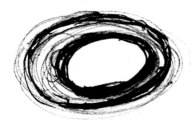

Matsunoyama
Natural Science Museum "Kyororo"

Located in the mountains of Matsunoyama, a region in the Niigata Prefecture known for its heavy winter snowfalls, "Kyororo" is a facility dedicated to educational and research activities in the field of natural science. The facility was planned to house both a permanent base for scientists and exhibition spaces for the general public. A great emphasis was put on incorporating the environment's natural and climatic features into the concept. The structure's pitched cross-section was inspired by the sheds that protect local roads from the snow and are common in the region. The floor plan, shaped like a snake, follows the pattern of the paths surrounding the site. "Kyororo …," the sound emitted by a local variety of kingfisher, gave the project its name.

The total length of the building, tower included, is 160 meters. With an outer shell entirely made of six-millimeter-thick welded corten steel plates, the difference in temperature between summer and winter causes the snake-like structure to expand and contract almost twenty centimeters in length. Snowfalls in the region often reach thirty meters per year and form snowdrifts of up to seven meters high, so the building has to withstand a total load of some 2,000 tons, as if it were a submarine buried under deep snow.

In the wintertime visitors are led through high walls of piled snow and enter a unique tunnel world, where they are shielded from the harsh climate. The width of the interior space reflects the movement of people within it, providing large spaces at angles where visitors pause to observe nature and becomes narrower where they

„Kyororo" ist eine Einrichtung zu naturwissenschaftlichen Lehr- und Forschungszwecken in den Bergen von Matsunoyama, einer Region in der Präfektur Niigata, die für ihre starken Schneefälle bekannt ist. Die Einrichtung soll Wissenschaftlern als Wirkungsstätte dienen sowie Ausstellungsräume für die allgemeine Öffentlichkeit beherbergen. Großer Wert wurde darauf gelegt, die natürlichen und klimatischen Bedingungen der Gegend in das Konzept mit einzubeziehen. Der steil ansteigende Querschnitt der Konstruktion leitet sich von der Form der Wetterdächer ab, die in dieser Region die Straßen vor den Schneemassen schützen. Der serpentinenartig gewundene Grundriss des Gebäudes spiegelt sich in der Form der Pfade wider, die sich um das Grundstück schlängeln. „Kyororo …", der Lockruf eines dort beheimateten Eisvogels, verlieh dem Projekt seinen Namen.

Die Gesamtlänge des Gebäudes beträgt einschließlich des Turmes 160 Meter. Die schlangenähnliche Konstruktion mit ihrer Außenhülle aus sechs Millimeter dicken zusammengeschweißten Corten-Stahlplatten kann sich durch die Temperaturunterschiede im Sommer und Winter um bis zu zwanzig Zentimeter in der Länge zusammenziehen oder ausdehnen. In der Region treten häufig Schneefälle von dreißig Metern pro Jahr auf, die Schneewehen von bis zu sieben Metern Höhe entstehen lassen. Ähnlich wie ein U-Boot unter Wasser muss das Gebäude unter dem Schnee einem Druck von ca. 2000 Tonnen standhalten können.

merely walk along. At key points inside the building, massive floor-to-ceiling windows give a spectacular view over the yukiguni ("snow country"). The largest of the 55- to 75-millimeter-thick acrylic windows measures 14.5 x 4 meters and weighs approximately four tons. Its degree of transparency is 98 percent. Visitors are thus able to fully admire the cross-sections of snow that are revealed, as well as the creatures living there. Apparently, just before the snow reaches the roof, a distinctive light can be seen filtering through the remaining gap at the top of the windows.

In summertime the large cross sections of snow are replaced by views of Buna trees and terraces for rice cultivation. The appearance of the weather-resistant steel outer shell changes with the passage of time. From the other side of the valley the building looks already like a ruin from the Inca period, with its tower giving the impression that it has dominated the treetops for aeons.

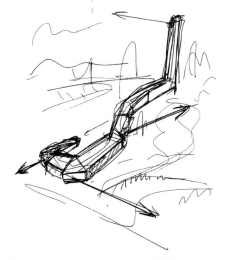

Zur Winterszeit eintreffende Besucher, die zwischen hohen Wällen aus aufgeschichtetem Schnee hindurchgeleitet werden, betreten eine einzigartige Tunnelwelt, in der sie vor dem eisigen Klima geschützt sind. Im Inneren ist die Breite des Gebäudes an die Bedürfnisse der Besucher angepasst: Aussichtspunkte bieten ausgedehnten Platz zum Verweilen und zur Betrachtung der Natur, das Gebäude verengt sich dort, wo man vorübergeht. Gewaltige Fenster, die vom Boden bis zur Decke reichen, bieten an zentralen Stellen spektakuläre Aussichten über das yukiguni („Schneeland"). Das größte der 55 bis 75 Millimeter dicken Acrylglasfenster misst 14,5 x 4 Meter und wiegt ca. vier Tonnen. Es hat eine Transparenz von 98 Prozent — Besucher können daher an den Fensterscheiben die Querschnitte der Schneewehen einschließlich der darin existierenden Tierwelt in vollem Umfang bestaunen. Kurz bevor die Schneewehe das Dach erreicht, entsteht ein unverwechselbares Licht, das von den letzten durch den winzigen verbliebenen Spalt an der Fensteroberseite scheinenden Lichtstrahlen erzeugt wird.

Wenn es Sommer wird, sind die Schneemassen verschwunden, und es bieten sich Ausblicke auf Buna-Bäume und Reisterrassenfelder. Im Laufe der Zeit verändert der wetterbeständige Stahl der Außenhülle sein Erscheinungsbild. Von der anderen Seite des Tals betrachtet, sieht das Gebäude schon jetzt wie eine Ruine aus der Inka-Zeit aus, sein Turm scheint bereits seit ewigen Zeiten die Baumwipfel zu überragen.

Eaves House

The house is located in a residential area just outside of Tokyo. The site is located on the edge of the flood plain beside a river and was converted into a residential area a long time ago. The river only exists as a stream along the western edge of the site. The western part of the site is situated lower than the level of the main site and the view from the house is directed primarily to the west.

There is no column at the southwest corner in order to maximize the openness to the wood deck, which extends to the edge of the site. The plan of the house is not square. Each of the walls is aligned parallel to the edge of the site. The entire site has been transformed into a house without any distinction between the garden and the house itself.

Das Haus befindet sich in einer Wohngegend etwas außerhalb Tokios. Das vor längerer Zeit mit einer Wohnsiedlung bebaute Areal ist am Rand des Überschwemmungsgebietes eines Flusses gelegen, an den heutzutage nur noch ein westlich der Siedlung verlaufender Bach erinnert. Der westliche Teil des Grundstücks liegt tiefer als der Hauptteil; der Blick vom Haus aus ist hauptsächlich nach Westen gerichtet.

Das Haus hat in der südwestlichen Ecke keine Stütze, um die Öffnung zu der bis an die Grundstücksgrenze reichenden Sonnenterrasse aus Holz zu maximieren. Der Grundriss des Hauses ist nicht quadratisch; alle Wände verlaufen parallel zu den Grundstücksgrenzen. Das gesamte Grundstück ist so ohne Trennung zwischen Garten und Gebäudeinneren komplett in ein Haus umgewandelt worden.

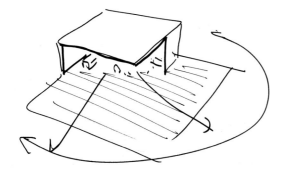

Cloister House

This is a house with a cloister for three children to run around in. A cloister in a monastery is a place for monks to move around while praying, but moving around is also an important activity for children. Running is the work of a child. Playing around is a good expression for this: for children, just running around can be playing.

If you stand in the courtyard garden, this outdoor area is not an extension of the indoor space but is an independent space. It could be just bare soil or the lush foliage of various plants whichever the inhabitants prefer, it establishes a contrast as an enclosed, controlled architectural space. The plan is for hamsters and beetles to live in the courtyard.

From inside the rooms you are very aware of the square formed by the thresholds and lintels going around the courtyard. The slight sense of unease you feel from the square is due to the fact there are no supporting columns at the four corners. Normally a square cloister is defined by a row of columns. Here the ceiling space enclosed by the spandrel walls gently produces a slight difference of quality between the interior and exterior spaces.

Dies ist ein Haus mit einem Kreuzgang, in dem drei Kinder umherlaufen und herumtoben können. In einem Kloster ist der Kreuzgang ein Ort, an dem die Mönche während der Andacht umhergehen. Aber auch für Kinder stellt das Herumlaufen eine wichtige Tätigkeit dar: Das Laufen ist die Arbeit des Kindes. „Herumspielen" ist ein passender Ausdruck dafür, denn auch bloßes Umherlaufen kann für Kinder ein Spiel sein.

Wenn man im Innenhofgarten steht, vermittelt sich dieser nicht als Erweiterung des Innenraumes, sondern als ein separater Raum. Ob schlichtweg mit Erde bedeckt, vom Laubwerk der unterschiedlichsten Pflanzen überwuchert oder was immer die Bewohner sonst vorziehen mögen – in jedem Fall stellt er einen Kontrast dar als ein umschlossener, domestizierter architektonischer Raum. Es ist geplant, dass zukünftig Hamster und Käfer im Innenhof leben.

Wenn man sich in den Innenräumen aufhält, ist man sich des Quadrats, das von den rings um den Innenhof herumführenden Bodenschwellen und Deckenabschlüssen gebildet wird, äußerst bewusst. Das leichte Gefühl des Unbehagens, das von diesem Quadrat ausgeht, entspringt der Tatsache, dass an den vier Ecken keine Stützpfeiler vorhanden sind. Normalerweise zeichnet sich ein quadratischer Kreuzgang durch Säulenreihen aus – hier deuten die Wandansätze im Deckenbereich dezent die Grenze zwischen Innen und Außen an.

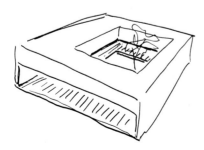

Atelier in Ushimado

"Please make spaces with good proportions," was the initial request. These instructions are reassuring for an architect. However, they are also rather difficult. Trying to create good proportions is a matter of course for architects, so this being particularly emphasized made us somewhat nervous.

The surrounding scenery is excellent. The port of Ushimado is below, and extending all around is a famously superb view. Mr. A is by no means an ordinary person. His former profession involved instigating large art-related projects, and he is also a member of a university arts faculty. Since his retirement he leads indeed a pleasant life. In order to create terraced fields, he is stacking up stonewalls one by one by hand. After placing a small, palm-sized radio on a corner of a stonewall,—on rainy days as well on sunny ones—he stacks up stones from morning to evening. There is a thoroughly mature aesthetic here.

Our situation was comparable to that of a food expert sitting and scowling in front of the counter, saying to the sushi chef, "please prepare well-balanced, utterly delicious tuna."

There is nothing in this house. To be more precise, the presence of objects that are not compatible with the spaces is not permitted. In the six-meter-high dining/living room there is only one huge, solid table. There is no sofa or bookshelf. Chairs are lined up along the table, but only on the side facing the view from the window. The alignment of the table commands a view over Ushimado Bay. The intention is to array artworks along the large wall, but at present it remains a completely

„Bitte gestalten Sie mir Räume mit guten Proportionen", lautete die ursprüngliche Bitte. Das hörten wir natürlich gerne – andererseits: Eine ausgewogene Proportionalität sollte für einen Architekten eigentlich eine Selbstverständlichkeit sein, daher machte uns die besondere Betonung dieser Thematik etwas nervös.

Die landschaftliche Umgebung ist exzellent. Unterhalb des Grundstücks liegt der Hafen von Ushimado, und in alle Richtungen eröffnen sich spektakuläre Aussichten. Herr A. der Auftraggeber, ist keine gewöhnliche Person. Früher beschäftigte er sich beruflich mit der Entwicklung groß angelegter künstlerischer Projekte; außerdem ist er Mitglied der Kunstfakultät einer Universität. Seit seiner Pensionierung gestaltet sich sein Leben angenehm: Er ist mit der Anlage terrassenförmiger Felder beschäftigt; mit seinen eigenen Händen baut er Mauern aus Steinen, eine nach der anderen. An sonnigen wie auch an regnerischen Tagen stellt er sein handtellergroßes Radio auf der Ecke einer Steinmauer ab und stapelt von morgens bis abends Steine. Dieser Ort hat eine konsequent durchdachte Ästhetik.

Unsere Situation ließ sich also mit der eines Küchenchefs vergleichen, an dessen Sushi-Theke ein bekannter Restaurantkritiker Platz genommen hat und nun mit finsterem Blick verlangt: „Bitte bereiten Sie mir einen ausgewogenen, besonders köstlichen Thunfisch zu."

In diesem Haus gibt es rein gar nichts. Um es präziser auszudrücken, die Anwesenheit von Gegenständen, die die Gesamtästhetik stören könnten, ist nicht gestattet. Das sechs Meter hohe Ess- und Wohnzimmer weist nichts außer einem großen, massiven Tisch auf.

empty white wall. Mr. A requested to eliminate the washbasin in the bathroom. The reason given was that when looking out from the bathtub, the washbasin would have been a visual obstruction. Instead, the washbasin was incorporated into the wall with which it is seamlessly unified. Unfortunately, the toilet could not be constructed in the same way and so remains in the space.

Our own specially designed wood-burning stove has also been embedded in the wall. Such a stove produces radiant heat, so it is usually placed in the middle of a space, but for Mr. A the overall visual impression was more important.

Es existiert kein Sofa oder Bücherregal. Am Tisch stehen einige Stühle, jedoch lediglich auf der dem Fenster zugewandten Seite. Die Ausrichtung des Tisches erlaubt den Ausblick über die Bucht von Ushimado. Es ist beabsichtigt, an der langen Wand Kunstwerke anzubringen, aber zurzeit sieht man noch eine völlig leere, weiße Wand. Herr A. bat uns, das Waschbecken aus dem Badezimmer zu entfernen: Ein Waschbecken würde den Blick von der Badewanne aus nach draußen stören. Das Waschbecken ist nun stattdessen in die Wand eingelassen und nahtlos in die Wandfläche integriert. Leider ließ sich die Toilette nicht auf ähnliche Weise eliminieren und verblieb daher im Raum.

Ebenfalls in die Wand eingebettet ist der von uns speziell entwickelte, mit Holz befeuerte Heizofen. Öfen dieser Art produzieren Strahlungshitze, sodass sie für gewöhnlich in der Raummitte platziert werden, doch für Herrn A. hatte der visuelle Eindruck Priorität.

GRV

This is an extremely thin-walled building constructed entirely of steel plates, creating an origami-like appearance. The client is a member of GRV, a famous graphic designers' group. Our aim was to create a design that was very simple but somehow also very different, just like GRV's designs.

The building is just a steel frame structure with columns and beams, but the dimensions of the individual elements are unusual. The thickness of the walls is only nine millimeters, and the columns are just small "ribs," almost non-existent. The "ribs" are designed to take vertical rather than horizontal loads. The irregular origami-like external wall is the principal element maintaining the building's stability. The joints between columns and beams are pin-joints almost as if components of a machine rather than architecture and are precise to under 0.3 millimeters. The stairs are secondary structural elements bracing part of the horizontal loads. The insulation is applied to the outside of the building and incorporated within the weatherproof material, at a total thickness of only 45 millimeters. There is nothing inside the building except structural elements.

Dies ist ein vollständig aus Stahlplatten gefertigtes Gebäude mit ungewöhnlich dünnen Wänden, das wie ein Origami anmutet. Der Bauherr gehört zu GRV, einer bekannten Gruppe von Grafikdesignern. In Übereinstimmung mit dem Design von GRV strebten wir einen schlichten, aber dennoch ungewöhnlichen Entwurf an.

Das Gebäude besteht aus einer Rahmenstruktur aus Stützen und Trägern, wobei die Abmessungen der einzelnen Elemente allerdings untypisch sind. Die Wandstärke beträgt nur neun Millimeter, und mit ihrer fast verschwindend geringen Dicke sind die Stützen eher als dünne „Rippen" zu bezeichnen. Die Konstruktion der „Rippen" ist auf vertikale und nicht auf horizontale Belastung ausgerichtet. Die Aussteifung des Gebäudes wird primär durch die unregelmäßige Faltung der Außenwände erzielt. Die Stützen und Träger sind durch Bolzen verbunden und weisen eine Toleranz von weniger als 0,3 Millimetern auf – eine eher im Maschinenbau und weniger in der Architektur übliche Praxis. Die Treppenläufe im Inneren dienen ebenfalls der Aussteifung und tragen einen Teil der Horizontallast. Mit einer Gesamtdicke von lediglich 45 Millimetern ist die Wärmedämmung in das witterungsbeständige Material an der Außenseite integriert. Das Gebäudeinnere besteht ausschließlich aus statisch wirksamen Komponenten.

Roof House

It was actually the client who had the idea of having lunch on top of the roof.

Located in the suburbs of Tokyo, the Roof House divides the living spaces between the ground floor and the entire roof. By maintaining a simple plan and utilizing a lightweight, yet earthquake-resistant structure, the house provides a visually generous and richly tactile space for the family. The thin roof, timber columns, and structural plywood panels allow for a flexible partitioned space and open up the view through the house and into the nearby valley and Mt. Kobo.

The partitioned spaces are also organized with eight skylights, one above each room, serving specific family members. Climbing up the ladders that can be leaned to the ledges of each skylight, the living space extends onto the rooftop and merges with the exterior. A freestanding wall exists as a windbreak and also provides privacy. The rooftop is equipped with a dining table, benches, a kitchen, a stove, and even a shower. The 1:10 pitched roof provides a comfortable slope identical to that of the original topography and has a low roof edge to further connect life on the roof to that of the garden, making it easy to serve barbecues from the

Die Idee stammte ursprünglich vom Bauherrn selbst, der den Traum hegte, auf dem Dach seines Hauses zu Mittag zu speisen.

Die Wohnräume des in einem Vorort Tokios angesiedelten Hauses befinden sich im Erdgeschoss und erstrecken sich zudem über die gesamte Dachfläche. Mit einem einfachen Grundriss und einer leichtgewichtigen, aber dennoch erdbebensicheren Konstruktion bietet das Haus der Familie visuell und taktil ansprechende Räumlichkeiten. Ein dünnes Dach und eine Konstruktion aus stützenden Holzbalken und Sperrholzplatten erlauben eine flexible Raumaufteilung und lassen den Blick ungehindert durch das gesamte Haus sowie über das nahe gelegene Tal bis zum Mt.-Kobo-Gebirge schweifen.

Jeder einzelne der acht Räume hat ein separates Fenster zum Dach, das jeweils einem bestimmten Familienmitglied zugedacht ist. Wenn man eine der Leitern hinaufklettert, die an die Fenstersimse gelehnt werden können, erweitert sich der Wohnraum bis hinaus auf die Dachoberfläche und bildet einen nahtlosen Übergang zum Außenraum. Als Windschutz dient eine freistehende Wand, die auch eine gewisse Privatsphäre bietet. Das Dach ist mit einem Esstisch, Bänken, einem Herd und sogar mit einer Dusche ausgestattet. Mit einer leichten Neigung im Verhältnis 1:10 weist es eine angenehme Schräglage auf, die identisch mit der ursprünglichen Topographie ist. Die niedrige Dachkante erlaubt die einfache Kommunikation zwischen Dach und Garten, wie zum Beispiel das mühelose Hinaufreichen von im Garten gegrilltem Fleisch.

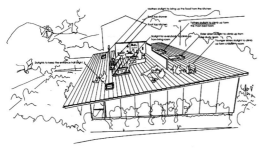

Toyota L&F Building

This is a both a facility for the maintenance of forklift trucks and an office. To comply with Toyota's existing concepts, a functional aesthetic was required.
Though a three-meter ceiling height was sufficient for the office, the maintenance area required nine meters. In combining these two functions, we pursued flexibility and at the same time attempted to create a particular spatial quality. The structure is a single framework utilizing 600-millimeter-deep steel beams. Absolutely no superfluous details or tension cables are used. With nothing more than this dense array of columns and beams—very similar to the Torii gates at the Inari Shrine—a simple space has been created. Horizontal rigidity is maintained by tie beams between the frames. Compared in scale to the 45-meter span, the 65-millimeter-thick roof and exterior walls are almost paper-thin.
We concentrated our creativity on the design of the sliding doors. In ordinary maintenance areas, oversliders and shutters are used, but the guide rails remain when they are opened. With sliding doors, nothing remains. The construction of the sliding doors (5.6 tons and 8 x 8 meters) were trusted to the company that manufactured the 80 meters high doors for the hangar at the Tanegashima Space Center.

*Dieser Bau beherbergt sowohl eine Gabelstaplerwerkstatt als auch die dazugehörigen Büros. Getreu der Identität des Unternehmens Toyota war eine funktionale Ästhetik gefordert. Obwohl für das Büro eine Deckenhöhe von drei Metern ausgereicht hätte, sollte die Wartungshalle eine Höhe von neun Metern aufweisen. Bei der Kombination der beiden Vorgaben arbeiteten wir auf eine flexible Lösung hin und versuchten zugleich, eine besondere räumliche Ästhetik zu schaffen.
Die Konstruktion besteht aus einem Gerüst aus 600 Millimeter tiefen Stahlträgern. Auf jedes überflüssige Detail wie auch auf Spannseile wurde verzichtet. Mit ausschließlich diesen Stützen und Trägern, die in ihrer dichten Aneinanderreihung an die Torii-Tore des Inari-Schreins in Kyoto erinnern, wurde ein einfacher Raum erzeugt. Die horizontale Stabilität wird durch Spannbalken zwischen den Dachträgern erreicht. Bei einer Spannweite von insgesamt 45 Metern sind das Dach und die Außenwände mit einem Querschnitt von 65 Millimetern – proportional betrachtet – so dünn wie Papier.
Unsere ganze Kreativität floss in die Konstruktion der Schiebetore. Für gewöhnlich werden in Wartungshallen Schiebetore mit Sandwichpaneelen oder Rolltore verwendet, wobei allerdings die Laufschienen stets sichtbar im Raum verbleiben, selbst wenn die Tore geöffnet sind. Bei Schiebetüren jedoch bleibt nichts Sichtbares zurück. Bei den 5,6 Tonnen schweren, 8 x 8 Meter großen Schiebetoren vertrauten wir auf eine Firma, die die 80 Meter hohen Tore für den Hangar des Tanegashima-Raumfahrtzentrums gefertigt hatte.*

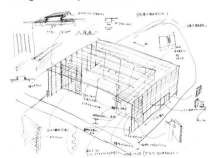

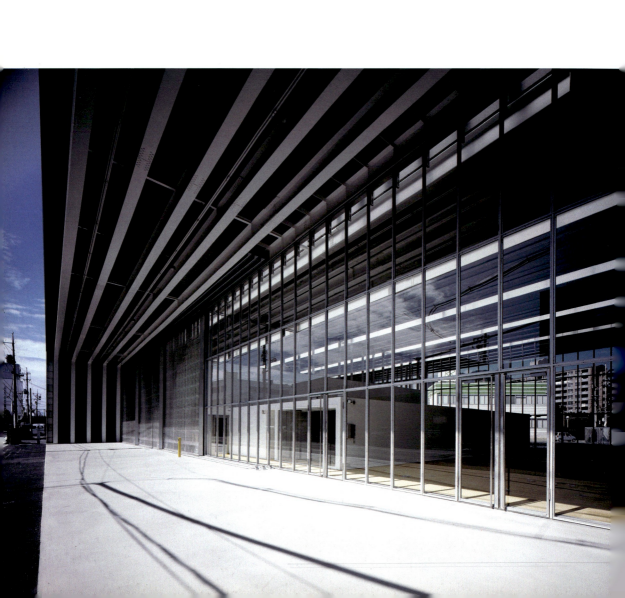

Wall-less House

This large site in a dense residential neighbourhood in Setagaya-ku district in Tokyo provides a rare opportunity to open the house completely to the landscape and environment, like a retreat villa in the countryside. Occupying only twenty percent of the site, the house leaves ample space around it for a truly open, continuous space, a wall-less house.

Using a lightweight steel load-bearing frame structure, the vertical loads are distributed through only a utility core in the center and two thin columns, therefore opening the living space to the outside completely on all sides. Thus, the floors seem to float in air, surrounded by the trees for greenery and privacy.

Dieses große, in einem dicht besiedelten Wohngebiet gelegene Grundstück im Setagaya-ku-Distrikt in Tokio bot die seltene Gelegenheit, ein Stadthaus vollständig der Landschaft und der Umgebung zu öffnen und in ein Refugium ganz im Stil einer Landhausvilla zu verwandeln. Das Grundstück, von dem das Haus lediglich zwanzig Prozent einnimmt, bietet ausreichend Platz für eine durchgängig offene Fläche – denn hier handelt es sich tatsächlich um ein Haus ohne Wände.

Die Vertikallast der leichtgewichtigen tragenden Stahlkonstruktion verteilt sich auf den Mittelschacht, in dem der versorgungstechnische Kern untergebracht ist, und nicht mehr als zwei dünne Stützpfeiler, wodurch eine vollständige Öffnung des Wohnraumes nach außen zu allen Seiten hin ermöglicht wird. Die Wohnebenen, die frei in der Luft zu schweben scheinen, sind von Bäumen umgeben, die Grün spenden und vor fremden Blicken schützen.

Floating Roof House

This house is located at the foot of a mountain. A dense forest grows in abundance to the rear, and at the edge of the site there are steps leading down and extending to a residential district of Okayama.

A thin roof was preferred in this case, as we wanted to create the effect of a single plane floating in the air, with the forested hills in the background extending right up to the edge of the site. When viewed from below, only the 40-meter-long and 160-millimeter-thick eaves line can be seen. The roof is supported by walls in only three places. It has a maximum projection of nine meters around the entry hall area.

Solid oak is used for the floors and walls. To avoid losing a sense of the presence of the oak, we deliberately allowed variations in thickness to remain, and pre-planned that a range of gaps would appear when humidity is low. The bathroom includes a bathtub and hand basin; the walls and the floor are faced with polished artificial stone creating a sense of unity.

Dieses Haus ist am Fuße eines Berges gelegen. Rückseitig schließt sich ein üppiger, dicht bewachsener Wald an, und am vorderen, abschüssigen Rand verbinden Stufen das Grundstück mit einem Wohngebiet in Okayama.

Bevorzugt wurde in diesem Fall ein dünnes Dach, da wir vor dem Hintergrund der dicht an das Grundstück heranreichenden bewaldeten Hügel die Wirkung einer einzelnen, in der Luft schwebenden Fläche erzielen wollten. Von unten betrachtet, ist einzig die 40 Meter lange und 160 Millimeter dicke Traufkante zu sehen. An lediglich drei Stellen wird das Dach von Wänden abgestützt. Die maximale Auskragung an der Eingangshalle beträgt neun Meter.

Für die Fußböden und Wände wurde massive Eiche verwendet. Um den besonderen Charakter des Holzes zu erhalten, ließen wir Variationen in der Stärke ganz bewusst zu und kalkulierten außerdem die Entstehung von Spalten bei niedriger Luftfeuchtigkeit mit ein. Im Bad, das mit einer Badewanne und einem Waschbecken ausgestattet ist, sind Wände und Fußboden mit dem gleichen polierten künstlichen Stein verkleidet, wodurch ein Gefühl von Einheitlichkeit vermittelt wird.

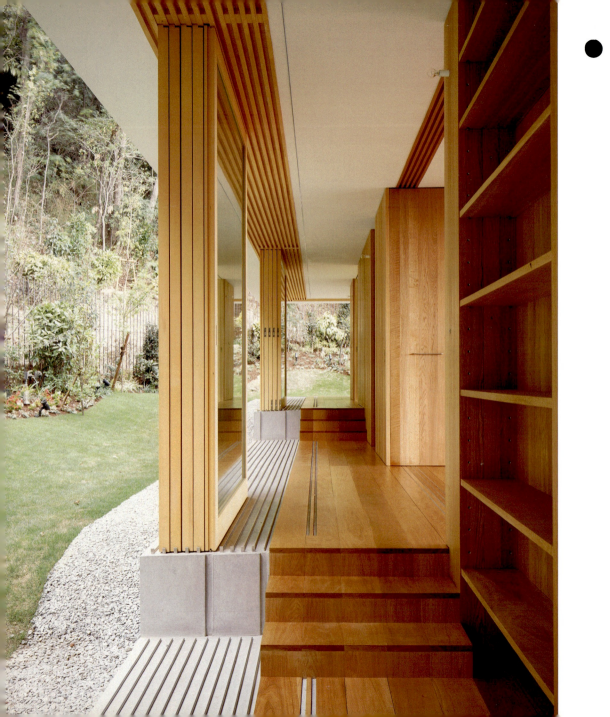

Megaphone House

This house consists entirely of a single 6 x 9 x 12 meter volume with a large opening at one end to capture the view of the sea and Enoshima Island. Except for storage on the lower level, the house is just one continuous space. When the partitions are retracted into their pockets, the space including the toilet and bathroom becomes a megaphone tube, extending from the back garden to the sea.

Various devices have been added to the enormous 6 x 9 meter glass surface. The vertically hung exterior blinds—primarily intended to block direct sunlight— become an awning for the lower level when articulated to project horizontally. The windows on the lower level comprise nine sliding panels. When opened from one end to the other, the boundaries between the horizon and the architectural space completely disappear. Located right in front of the glass façade, a wood-burning stove we designed especially for the space enhances the view towards the sea; particularly in the evening, it provides heating for the family without obstructing the night view.

Dieses Haus besteht aus einem einzigen 6 x 9 x 12 Meter großen Volumen; es hat an der zum Ozean liegenden Seite eine große Öffnung, die den Blick auf das Meer und die Insel Enoshima erschließt. Mit Ausnahme eines Abstellraumes auf der unteren Ebene bildet das gesamte Haus eine durchgängig offene Fläche. Sind die Trennwände zurückgeschoben und in ihren Gehäusen verschwunden, verwandelt sich der Raum einschließlich der Toilette und des Bades in ein vom Hintergarten zum Meer gerichtetes gigantisches Megafon.

Die sechs mal neun Meter große Fensterfront aus Glas wurde mit verschiedenem Zubehör versehen. Die außen angebrachten Blenden dienen in vertikaler Ausrichtung dem Zweck, den Innenraum vor direktem Sonnenlicht abzuschirmen; sie können jedoch auch horizontal nach außen gestellt werden und lassen sich somit zu einer Markise zum Schutz der unteren Wohnebene umfunktionieren. Auf der unteren Ebene bestehen die Fenster aus neun Schiebepaneelen. Wenn diese von einem Ende zum anderen durchgehend geöffnet sind, ist die Scheidewand, die den architektonischen Raum von der bis zum Horizont reichenden Weite trennt, komplett verschwunden. Unmittelbar vor der Glasfassade platziert, unterstreicht ein speziell von uns entwickelter, mit Holz befeuerter Ofen den Blick auf das Meer; besonders abends spendet er Wärme, ohne jedoch die nächtliche Aussicht der Familie zu stören.

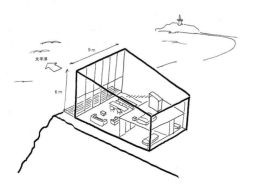

Engawa House

The Engawa House was designed to accommodate a family. To the north of the site is the grandparents' home, with the eldest son and his family living on the second floor, and adjacent is the building where the eldest son and his wife manage a construction company. The building-to-land ratio in the area is high and the footprint of most houses takes up the entire property, leaving no space for a garden.

The grandparents' home was no exception, with its southern engawa—a typical Japanese multifunctional space similar to the veranda—facing a large wall only fifty centimeters away. The border to the southern lot where their daughter and her husband, who are uninvolved in the family business, decided to settle when by chance it went on sale.

Plans were thus laid out for a long and narrow building bordering the south road. An open area along the northern side provides space for an inner garden, which a single-storey house would allow enough light for. The southern roadside wall was erected to a height of 2.2 meters, with a high side opening that while still protecting the family's privacy, would provide a clear view of the sky. On the other side, floor-to-ceiling windows provide a full view of the garden. The result is a 16.2-meter-long and 4.6-meter-wide space encased between two L-shaped frames.

Nine sliding doors allow the house to be opened up completely on the garden side. And so when fifty people, both family and friends, gathered at a garden party to celebrate the completion of the building, they

Das Engawa House wurde für eine Familie entworfen. Nördlich an das Grundstück grenzt das Wohnhaus der Großeltern, in dem auf der zweiten Etage auch der älteste Sohn mit seiner Familie wohnt, und anliegend ist das Gebäude, in dem dieser mit seiner Frau ein Bauunternehmen betreibt. Die Gegend ist dicht besiedelt, und die meisten Gebäude nehmen mit ihrer Grundfläche das gesamte Grundstück ein, sodass kein Platz für einen Garten übrig ist.

Das Haus der Großeltern mit seinem engawa auf der Südseite – einem typisch japanischen multifunktionalen Raum, vergleichbar mit einer Veranda – bildete in dieser Hinsicht keine Ausnahme. Gegenüber, in nur fünfzig Zentimeter Entfernung, gab es eine Trennwand, die die Grenze zu eben jenem südlichen Baugrundstück bildete, auf dem sich die Tochter und ihr Ehemann, die beide nicht in dem Familienunternehmen tätig sind, niederließen, als das Areal zufällig zum Verkauf angeboten wurde.

Es wurden Pläne für ein langes, schmales Gebäude erstellt, das an die südlich gelegene Straße angrenzen sollte. Eine Freifläche an der nördlichen Längsseite bot Platz für den Garten, der wegen des niedrigen einstöckigen Hauses ausreichend Licht erhält. Die zur Straßenseite gelegene südliche Wand ist 2,20 Meter hoch und hat eine hohe seitliche Öffnung, die ungehindert in den Himmel blicken lässt, während gleichzeitig die Privatsphäre der Familie geschützt bleibt. Auf der anderen Seite bieten vom Boden bis zur Decke reichende Fenster Aussicht über den gesamten Garten. Das Ergebnis ist ein Raum von 16,20 Meter Länge und

naturally came up with the idea that the whole structure resembles an engawa, architecturally speaking this sort of long compartment is not a classic example of an engawa, but the idea certainly makes sense.

4,60 Metern Breite mit einem Rahmen aus zwei L-förmigen Trägerelementen.

Insgesamt neun Schiebetüren öffnen das Haus zur Gartenseite hin komplett. Als fünfzig Freunde und Verwandte der Familie im Garten zusammenkamen, um die Hauseinweihungsparty zu feiern, entstand die ganz natürliche Vorstellung, dass der gesamte Bau einem engawa ähnlich sei. Sicherlich handelt es sich aus architektonischer Sicht bei einem solchen länglichen Raum nicht um ein klassisches Beispiel, aber trotzdem leuchtet die Idee ein.

Plans *Pläne*

Floor Plans
Grundrisse

Sections
Schnitte

Elevations
Ansichten

Scale
Maßstab
1:400

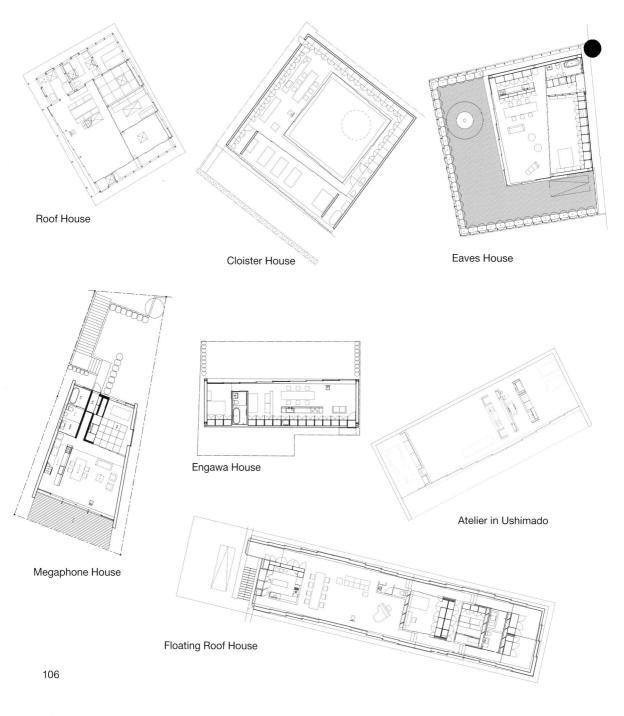

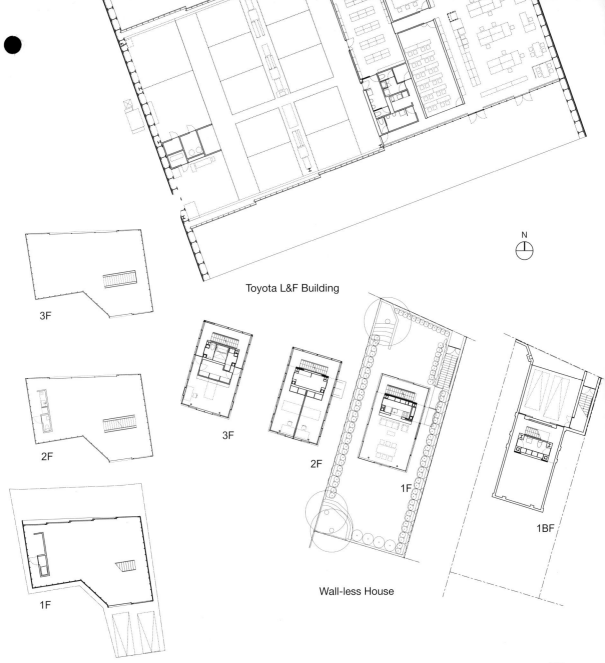

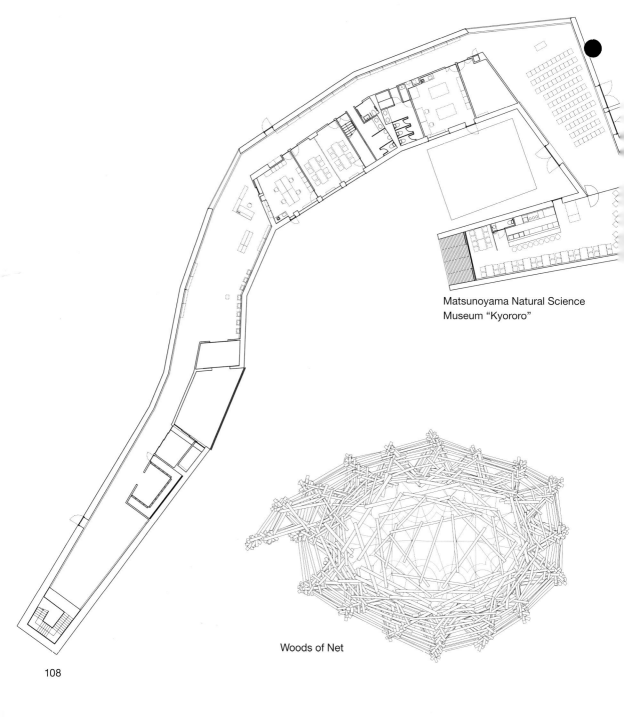

Matsunoyama Natural Science Museum "Kyororo"

Woods of Net

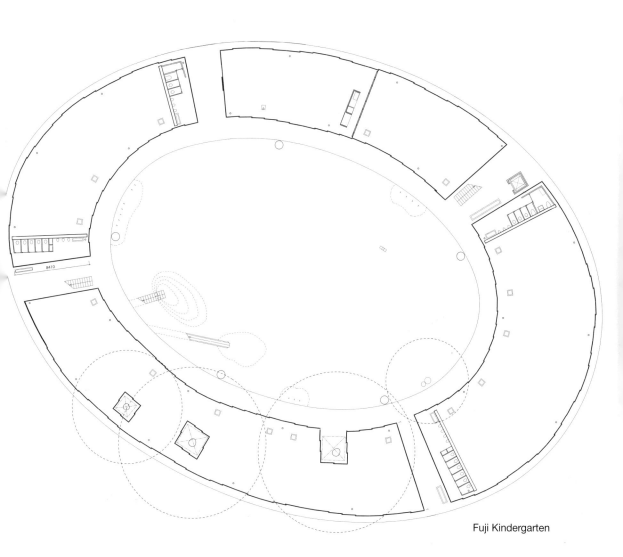

Fuji Kindergarten

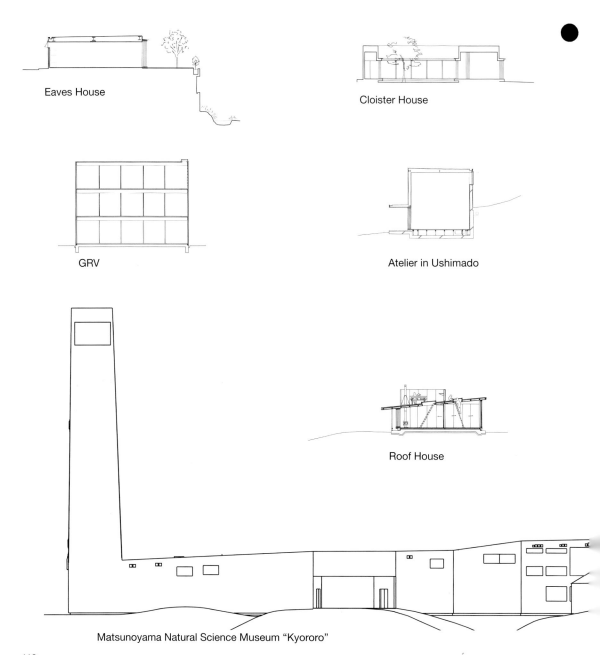

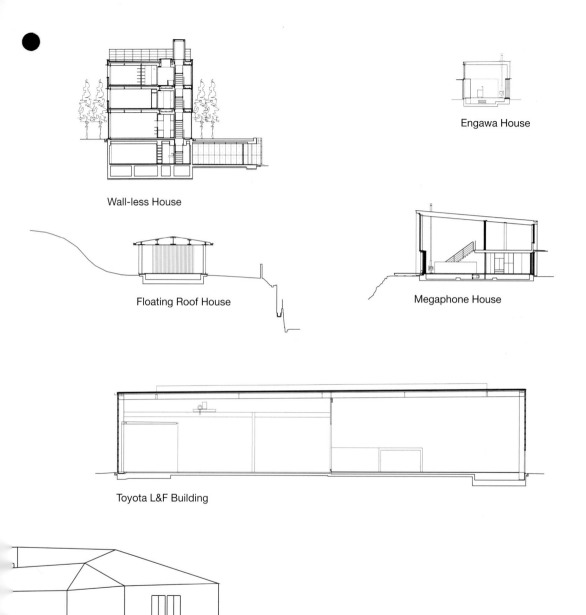

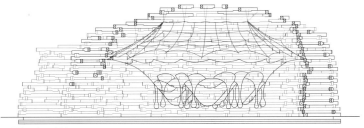

Woods of Net

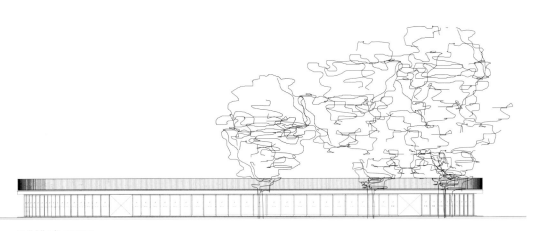

Fuji Kindergarten

Supplement *Anhang*

List of Works
Werkverzeichnis

Biography Tezuka Architects
Biografie Tezuka Architects

Contributors
Autoren

Imprint Exhibition
Impressum Ausstellung

List of Works *Werkverzeichnis*

PROJECT NUMBER, PROJECT NAME
1. PRINCIPAL USE, BUILDING SITE
2. SITE AREA, BUILDING AREA, TOTAL FLOOR AREA
3. NUMBER OF STOREYS, TYPE OF STRUCTURE S: STEEL, RC: REINFORCED CONCRETE, W: WOOD
4. ARCHITECTS
5. DESIGN PERIOD, CONSTRUCTION PERIOD

PROJEKTNUMMER, PROJEKTNAME
1. *NUTZUNG, ORT*
2. *GRUNDSTÜCKSFLÄCHE, GRUNDFLÄCHE, BRUTTOGESCHOSSFLÄCHE*
3. *ANZAHL DER GESCHOSSE, BAUWEISE S: STAHL, RC: STAHLBETON, W: HOLZ*
4. *ARCHITEKTEN*
5. *ENTWURFSZEITRAUM, BAUZEIT*

01 Soejima Hospital
1. Hospital, Saga-shi, Saga
2. 2227.01 m², 1415.62 m², 4079.48 m²
3. 4F, S
4. Takaharu + Yui Tezuka
5. 1994.7–1995.5, 1995.3–1996.3

02 Cherry Blossom House
1. Residence
2. 82.54 m², 40.42 m², 40.42 m²
3. 1F, RC
4. Takaharu + Yui Tezuka
5. 1996.8

03 Wood Deck House
1. Residence, Kamakura-shi, Kanagawa
2. 269.15 m², 67.28 m², 128.45 m²
3. 3F, S
4. Takaharu + Yui Tezuka, Masahiro Ikeda, Kentaro Shono
5. 1998.1–1998.12, 1999.2–1999.8

04 Light Gauge Steel House
1. Residence, Fujisawa-shi, Kanagawa
2. 112.90 m², 46.37 m², 139.11 m²
3. 3F, S + LGS
4. Takaharu + Yui Tezuka, Masahiro Ikeda, Kentaro Shono, Makoto Takei
5. 1998.4–1998.12, 1999.6–1999.10

05 Kawagoe Music Apartment
1. Collective Housing, Kawagoe-shi, Saitama
2. 522.55 m², 326.69 m², 2532.22 m²
3. B1F, 14F, SRC + RC
4. Takaharu + Yui Tezuka, Makoto Takei, Chie Nabeshima, Hiroshi Hibio, Tetsuya Yamazaki
5. 1998.4–1998.11, 1999.1–2000.2

06 Machiya House
1. Residence, Hachioji-shi, Tokyo
2. 227.20 m², 90.85 m², 90.85 m²
3. B1F, 1F, RC + S
4. Takaharu + Yui Tezuka, Masahiro Ikeda, Chie Nabeshima
5. 1998.9–1999.6, 1999.12–2000.7

07 Megaphone House
1. Residence, Kamakura-shi, Kanagawa
2. 264.18 m², 103.96 m², 157.18 m²
3. 2F, S
4. Takaharu + Yui Tezuka, Masahiro Ikeda, Makoto Takei
5. 2000.1–2000.6, 2000.7–2000.11

08 Roof House
1. Residence, Hatano-shi, Kanagawa
2. 298.59 m², 107.65 m², 96.89 m²
3. 1F, W
4. Takaharu + Yui Tezuka, Masahiro Ikeda
5. 2000.3–2000.8, 2000.9–2001.3

09 Balcony House
1. Residence + Shop & Cafe, Miura-gun, Kanagawa
2. 124.12 m², 44.26 m², 129.28 m²
3. 3F, S
4. Takaharu + Yui Tezuka, Masahiro Ikeda, Chie Nabeshima
5. 2000.6–2000.12, 2001.1–2001.6

10 Wall-less House
1. Residence, Setagaya-ku, Tokyo
2. 255.19 m², 50.84 m², 239.91 m²
3. B1F, 3F, S
4. Takaharu + Yui Tezuka, Makoto Takei
5. 2000.1–2000.6, 2000.4–2000.12

11 House to Catch the Sky
1. Residence, Kawasaki-shi, Kawasaki
2. 173.20 m², 86.58 m², 86.58 m²
3. 1F, W + S
4. Takaharu + Yui Tezuka, Masahiro Ikeda, Wataru Obase
5. 2000.4–2000.10, 2001.2–2001.8

12 Step House
1. Residence, Atami-shi, Shizuoka
2. 386.71 m², 154.22 m², 205.97 m²
3. B1F, 2F, RC + S
4. Takaharu + Yui Tezuka, Masahiro Ikeda, Chie Nabeshima
5. 2000.4–2001.2, 2001.4–2001.12

13 House to Catch the Sky II
1. Residence, Suginami-ku, Tokyo
2. 74.32 m², 37.04 m², 74.08 m²
3. 2F, S
4. Takaharu + Yui Tezuka, Masahiro Ikeda, Makoto Takei
5. 2001.1–2001.7, 2001.8–2002.4

14 Anthill House
1. Residence, Suginami-ku, Tokyo
2. 53.75 m², 37.41 m², 156.43 m²
3. B1F, 4F, SRC
4. Takaharu + Yui Tezuka, Masahiro Ikeda, Takashi Kobayashi, Chie Nabeshima, Mayumi Miura
5. 2000.4–2001.5, 2001.6–2002.4

15 Thin Roof Sukiya
1. Residence, Kamakura-shi, Kanagawa
2. 250.74 m², 44.74 m², 44.74 m²
3. 1F, W
4. Takaharu + Yui Tezuka, Masahiro Ikeda, Takashi Kobayashi, Chie Nabeshima, Mayumi Miura
5. 2000.9–2000.12, 2001.1–2001.4

16 Thin Wall House
1. Residence, Shibuya-ku, Tokyo
2. 187.36 m², 68.80 m², 217.51 m²
3. B1F, 3F, S
4. Takaharu + Yui Tezuka, Masahiro Ikeda, Makoto Takei, Hiroshi Tomikawa
5. 2000.11–2001.11, 2001.12–2002.09

17 Hounancho "L" condominium
1. Residence, Suginami-ku, Tokyo
2. 513.14 m², 318.97 m², 1040.34 m²
3. B1F, 7F, RC
4. Takaharu + Yui Tezuka, Masahiro Ikeda, Wataru Obase
5. 2001.2–2001.9, 2001.10–2002.8

18 Canopy House
1. Residence, Chofu-shi, Tokyo
2. 187.36 m², 68.80 m², 116.32 m²
3. 2F, S
4. Takaharu + Yui Tezuka, Masahiro Ikeda, Akiyoshi Takagi
5. 2001.6–2002.2, 2002.4–2002.11

19 Saw Roof House
1. Residence, Ohta-ku, Tokyo
2. 281.25 m², 90.60 m², 181.20 m²
3. 2F, S
4. Takaharu + Yui Tezuka, Masahiro Ikeda, Chie Nabeshima
5. 2001.11–2002.5, 2002.6–2002.11

20 Skylight House
1 Residence, Kamakura-shi, Kanagawa
2 101.54 m², 60.83 m², 119.98 m²
3 2F, S
4 Takaharu + Yui Tezuka, Masahiro Ikeda, Ryuya Maio
5 2002.1–2002.8, 2002.9–2003.3

21 House to Catch the Sky III
1 Residence, Wako-shi, Saitama
2 150.00 m², 89.27 m², 89.27 m²
3 1F, W
4 Takaharu + Yui Tezuka, Masahiro Ikeda, Wataru Obase, Daijiro Nakayama
5 2002.4–2002.10, 2002.11–2003.4

22 Matsunoyama
Natural Science Museum "Kyororo"
1 Research Facility, Tokamachi-shi, Niigata
2 4269.15 m², 997.45 m², 1248.18 m²
3 B1F, 2F, S
4 Takaharu + Yui Tezuka, Masahiro Ikeda, Makoto Takei, Hiroshi Tomikawa, Ryuya Maio, Masafumi Harada, Miyoko Fujita, Mayumi Miura, Taro Suwa, Takahiro Nakano, Toshio Nishi, Tomohiro Sato
5 2001.8–2002.2, 2002.3–2003.6

23 Toyota L&F Building
1 Office & Maintenance Facility, Hiroshima-shi, Hiroshima
2 2965.98 m², 1504.28 m², 1504.28 m²
3 1F, S
4 Takaharu + Yui Tezuka, Masahiro Ikeda, Wataru Obase
5 2002.8–2003.5, 2003.5–2003.10

24 Engawa House
1 Residence, Adachi-ku, Tokyo
2 196.27 m², 74.48 m², 74.48 m²
3 1F, W + S
4 Takaharu + Yui Tezuka, Masahiro Ikeda, Chie Nabeshima, Mayumi Miura
5 2003.1–2003.5, 2003.5–2003.11

25 House to Catch the Sky IV
1 Residence, Chigasaki-shi, Kanagawa
2 259.04 m², 103.12 m², 103.12 m²
3 1F, W
4 Takaharu + Yui Tezuka, Masahiro Ikeda, Ryuya Maio
5 2002.7–2003.4, 2003.5–2003.12

26 Floating house
1 Residence, Meguro-ku, Tokyo
2 98.97 m², 51.03 m², 101.93 m²
3 B1F, 2F, S
4 Takaharu + Yui Tezuka, Masahiro Ikeda, Wataru Obase
5 2002.3–2002.12, 2003.4–2004.12

27 Five Courtyard House 5
1 Residence
2 277.22 m², 166.33 m², 220.91 m²
3 B1F, 1F, RC
4 Takaharu + Yui Tezuka, Masahiro Ikeda, Chie Nabeshima
5 2001.4–2003.4, 2003.6–2004.1

28 Thin Wall Office
1 Office, Shibuya-ku, Tokyo
2 120.40 m², 71.48 m², 283.51 m²
3 B1F, 3F, S
4 Takaharu + Yui Tezuka, Masahiro Ikeda, Hiroshi Tomikawa, Masafumi Harada
5 2002.8–2003.4, 2003.4–2004.2

29 Clipping Corner House
1 Residence, Kamakura-shi, Kanagawa
2 314.06 m², 106.85 m², 94.71 m²
3 1F, RC
4 Takaharu + Yui Tezuka, Masahiro Ikeda, Makoto Takei
5 2003.3–2003.9, 2003.10–2004.3

30 Double Courtyard House 2
1 Residence
2 853.96 m², 296.51 m², 237.21 m²
3 1F, S
4 Takaharu + Yui Tezuka, Masahiro Ikeda, Wataru Obase, Nana Nishimuta
5 2002.9–2003.8, 2003.9–2004.5

31 House to Catch the Forest
1 Weekend House, Chino-shi, Nagano
2 1054.10 m², 80.74 m², 80.74 m²
3 1F, W
4 Takaharu + Yui Tezuka, Masahiro Ikeda, Ryuya Maio
5 2003.4–2003.9, 2003.10–2004.4

32 Observatory House
1 Residence, Kamakura-shi, Kanagawa
2 136.50 m², 54.45 m², 175.09 m²
3 B1F, 3F, S + RC
4 Takaharu + Yui Tezuka, Masahiro Ikeda, Chie Nabeshima, Mayumi Miura
5 2003.1–2003.9, 2003.10–2004.7

33 Jyubako House
1 Residence, Setagaya-ku, Tokyo
2 100.01 m², 59.72 m², 136.55 m²
3 3F, RC
4 Takaharu + Yui Tezuka, Masahiro Ikeda, Akiyoshi Takagi
5 2003.1–2003.6, 2004.3–2004.10

34 Big Window House
1 Residence, Yokohama-shi, Kanagawa
2 85.07 m², 47.50 m², 95.00 m²
3 2F, W
4 Takaharu + Yui Tezuka, Masahiro Ikeda, Chie Nabeshima, Daisuke Kamijo
5 2003.12–2004.4, 2004.5–2004.11

35 Shoe Box House
1 Residence, Setagaya-ku, Tokyo
2 165.31 m², 82.65 m², 159.38 m²
3 3F, S + RC
4 Takaharu + Yui Tezuka, Masahiro Ikeda, Akiyoshi Takagi, Masafumi Harada
5 2003.8–2004.5, 2004.6–2004.12

36 Floating Roof House
1 Residence, Okayama
2 1035.92 m², 288.64 m², 342.70 m²
3 1F, RC + S
4 Takaharu + Yui Tezuka, Masahiro Ikeda, Chie Nabeshima, Hiroshi Tomikawa
5 2004.4–2004.12, 2005.1–2005.8

37 Roof Deck House
1 Residence
2 290.95 m², 137.25 m², 307.15 m²
3 B1F, 2F, RC + S
4 Takaharu + Yui Tezuka, Masahiro Ikeda, Chie Nabeshima, Asako Kompal
5 2004.2–2004.12, 2004.12–2005.10

38 Fuji Kindergarten
1 Kindergarten, Tachikawa, Tokyo
2 4791.69 m², 1419.25 m², 1304.01 m²
3 1F, S
4 Takaharu + Yui Tezuka, Masahiro Ikeda, Chie Nabeshima, Ryuya Maio, Asako Konparu, Kosuke Suzuki, Naoto Murakaji, Shigefumi Araki, Shuichi Sakuma, Masafumi Harada
5 2005.2–2006.3 / 2006.3–2006.9 (phase I), 2006.7–2007.1 (phase II)

39 Visionary Arts, Tokyo
1: Special Training School, Shibuya, Tokyo
2 655.10 m², 489.25 m², 3609.25 m²
3 B1F, 8F, S + RC + SRC
4 Takaharu + Yui Tezuka, Wataru Obase, Hiroshi Tomikawa, Akiyoshi Takagi, Shigefumi Araki, Shuichi Sakuma
5 2003.7–2003.12, 2004.1–2005.12

40 Eaves House
1 Residence, Saitama, Saitama
2 297.61 m², 119.57 m², 119.57 m²
3 1F, S
4 Takaharu + Yui Tezuka, Masahiro Ikeda, Ryuya Maio
5 2004.6–2005.5, 2005.6–2006.3

41 Observatory Room House
1 Residence, Yokohama, Kanagawa
2 109.62 m², 46.21 m², 92.42 m²
3 2F, W
4 Takaharu + Yui Tezuka, Masahiro Ikeda, Akiyoshi Takagi, Naoto Murakaji
5 2004.8–2005.7, 2005.8–2006.3

42 Studio to Catch the Sky
1 Residence, Suginami, Tokyo
2 105.01 m², 54.65 m², 109.30 m²
3 2F, W
4 Takaharu + Yui Tezuka, Masahiro Ikeda, Ryuya Maio, Kosuke Suzuki
5 2004.12–2005.10, 2005.11–2006.5

43 Sandou House
1 Residence, Hatsukaichi, Hiroshima
2 162.15 m², 96.11 m², 118.20 m²
3 2F, RC
4 Takaharu + Yui Tezuka, Masahiro Ikeda, Chie Nabeshima, Shigefumi Araki
5 2005.2–2005.10, 2005.11–2006.7

44 My Own Sky House
1 Residence, Ota, Tokyo
2 179.07 m², 107.13 m², 138.32 m²
3 B1F, 1F, RC + S
4 Takaharu + Yui Tezuka, Masahiro Ikeda, Akiyoshi Takagi, Naoto Murakaji
5 2004.9–2005.11, 2005.12–2006.8

45 House to Catch the Sunlight
1 Residence, Setagaya, Tokyo
2 95.88 m², 42.58 m², 82.16 m²
3 2F, W
4 Takaharu + Yui Tezuka, Hirofumi Ohno, Masafumi Harada, Shuichi Sakuma
5 2006.1–2006.6, 2006.7–2007.1

46 Temple to Catch the Hill
1 Temple, Living quarters, Yokohama, Kanagawa
2 596.13 m², 240.37 m², 357.62 m²
3 2F, W
4 Takaharu + Yui Tezuka, Katsuya Ikeda (Architecture Design of Ikeda), Masafumi Harada, Shuichi Sakuma, Hiroko Nakamura / AOI
5 2005.4–2006.5, 2006.6–2007.3

47 Cloister House
1 Residence, Ageo, Saitama
2 322.52 m², 148.33 m², 148.33 m²
3 1F, W
4 Takaharu + Yui Tezuka, Hirofumi Ohno, Ryuya Maio, Shoko Wakami
5 2006.5–2006.9, 2006.10–2007.6

48 High Ceiling Town House
1 Residence, Bunkyo, Tokyo
2 75.85 m², 52.01 m², 132.94 m²
3 3F, S
4 Takaharu + Yui Tezuka, Hirofumi Ohno, Ryuya Maio
5 2006.1–2006.12, 2006.12–2007.7

49 Kumejima Eef Beach Hotel
1 Hotel, Kumejima, Okinawa
2 28064.94 m², 2718.03 m² (renovation area), 5374.46 m² (renovation area)
3 3F
4 Takaharu + Yui Tezuka, Hirofumi Ohno, Naoto Murakaji, Atsushi Nozawa, Shin Hirayama, Hisako Yamamura
5 2006.10–2007.4, 2007.5–2007.10

50 House to Catch the Hill
1 Residence, Nagoya, Aichi
2 307.11 m², 68.40 m², 112.82 m²
3 B1F, 1F, RC
4 Takaharu + Yui Tezuka, Hirofumi Ohno, Shigefumi Araki, Hisako Yamamura
5 2006.7–2006.12, 2007.1–2007.10

51 Atelier in Ushimado
1 Residence, Setouchi, Okayama
2 918.38 m², 195.80 m², 151.80 m²
3 1F, S + RC
4 Takaharu + Yui Tezuka, Hirofumi Ohno, Shuichi Sakuma
5 2006.9–2007.5, 2007.6–2007.12

52 House to Catch the Sea
1 Residence, Chigasaki, Kanagawa
2 117.40 m², 51.54 m², 103.08 m²
3 2F, W + S
4 Takaharu + Yui Tezuka, Hirofumi Ohno, Ryuya Maio
5 2006.6–2007.3, 2007.5–2007.12

53 Cooperative House in Yuigahama
1 Row House, Kamakura, Kanagawa
2 294.10 m², 173.29 m², 530.38 m²
3 3F, RC
4 Takaharu + Yui Tezuka, Hirofumi Ohno, Ryuya Maio, Shoko Wakami
5 2006.3–2007.12, 2008.1–2008.12

54 GRV
1 Residence, Setagaya, Tokyo
2 184.77 m², 93.26 m², 279.78 m²
3 3F, S
4 Takaharu + Yui Tezuka, Hirofumi Ohno, Masafumi Harada, Kosuke Suzuki
5 2006.4–2007.6, 2008.7–2009.2

55 Singapore Bungalows
1 Cluster Housing, Singapore
2 3377 m², 1350 m², 5103 m²
3 B2F, 2F, RC
4 Takaharu + Yui Tezuka, UNIVERSAL AKITEK (Co-Architect), Ryuya Maio, Naoto Murakaji, Midori Taki
5 2008.6–2009.6, 2009.7–2011.3

56 Woods of Net, Hakone Open-Air Museum
1 Art, Hakone, Kanagawa
2 536.98 m², 536.98 m²
3 1F, W
4 Takaharu + Yui Tezuka, Norihide Imagawa, Ryuya Maio, Yusuke Fujita, Shoko Wakami, Sho Hamakawa
5 2008.5–2009.1, 2009.1–2009.5

Biography
Biografie

Takaharu Tezuka

1964	Born / *geboren* in Tokyo
1987	B. Arch., Musashi Institute of Technology
1990	M. Arch., University of Pennsylvania
1990–94	Richard Rogers Partnership Ltd.
1994	Established / *gründet* Tezuka Architects
1996–03	Assistant Professor, Musashi Institute of Technology
2003–	Associate Professor, Musashi Institute of Technology
2005, 06	Visiting Professor, Salzburg Summer Academy
2006	Visiting Professor, University of California, Berkeley
2009	Professor, Tokyo City University

Yui Tezuka

1969	Born / *geboren* in Kanagawa
1992	B. Arch., Musashi Institute of Technology
1992–93	The Bartlett School of Architecture, University College of London
1994	Established / *gründet* Tezuka Architects
1999–	Visiting Faculty, Toyo University
2001–	Visiting Faculty, Tokai University
2006	Visiting Professor, Salzburg Summer Academy
2006	Visiting Professor, University of California, Berkeley

Awards *Preise*

1997	Ministry of International Trade and Industry, Good Design Gold Prize (Soejima Hospital)
1998	Architectural Institution of Japan, Annual Architectural Commendations (Soejima Hospital)
2002	Japan Institute of Architects Prize (Roof House)
2003	Architectural Institution of Japan, Annual Architectural Commendations (Roof House)
2005	Architectural Institution of Japan, Annual Architectural Commendations (Matsunoyama Natural Science Museum)
2007	Ministry of Economy, Trade and Industry, Interaction Design Prize (Fuji Kindergarten)
	Ministry of Economy, Trade and Industry, Kids Design Gold Prize (Fuji Kindergarten)
	Association for Children's Enviroment, ACE Award Design Category (Fuji Kindergarten)
	Design for Asia Grand Award (Fuji Kindergarten)
2008	Architectural Institution of Japan Prize (Fuji Kindergarten)

Contributors *Autoren*

Paul Andreas

Art historian, architecture and design journalist, since 2007 press officer at the Deutsches Architekturmuseum (DAM), Frankfurt. Author of numerous articles, radio and TV features on architecture and design, in particular on the Japanese scene. Lives in Dusseldorf.

Kunsthistoriker, Architektur- und Designjournalist, seit 2007 Presse- und Öffentlichkeitsarbeit für das Deutsche Architekturmuseum (DAM), Frankfurt am Main. Autor zahlreicher Artikel, von Radio- und TV-Features zu Architektur und Design, unter anderem zur japanischen Szene. Lebt in Düsseldorf.

Joseph Grima

New York-based architect and researcher. After graduating from the Architectural Association in London, he worked as an editor and adviser at "Domus" magazine. He is at present Director of the Storefront for Art and Architecture in New York City and a regular contributor to a wide range of international publications.

Architekt und Wissenschaftler aus New York. Nach dem Abschluss an der Architectural Association in London arbeitete er als Redakteur und Berater bei der Zeitschrift „Domus". Zurzeit ist er Direktor der Storefront Gallery for Art and Architecture in New York City und ein regelmäßiger Mitarbeiter bei einer Reihe von internationalen Publikationen.

Taro Igarashi

Born in 1967 in Paris. Doctor of Engineering from University of Tokyo. Currently Associate Professor at Tohoku University. He was the commissioner of the Japanese pavilion of the 11th International Architecture Exhibition, Venice Biennale (2008). Author of numerous articles on Japanese architecture. Lives and works in Tokyo and Sendai.

1967 in Paris geboren. Doktor der Ingenieurwissenschaft an der Universität Tokio. Zurzeit außerordentlicher Professor an der Tohoku Universität. 2008 Generalkommissar des japanischen Pavillons auf der 11. Internationalen Architekturbiennale Venedig. Autor zahlreicher Veröffentlichungen über japanische Architektur. Lebt und arbeitet in Tokio und Sendai.

Imprint Exhibition *Impressum Ausstellung*

CURATOR / COORDINATOR Paul Andreas

CONCEPT Peter Cachola Schmal, Takaharu + Yui Tezuka, Paul Andreas

EXHIBITION DESIGN Takaharu + Yui Tezuka, Kai Kasugai, Matthias Neuendorf, Midori Taki (Tezuka Architects)

REALISATION Mario Lorenz (Deserve) with Gebrüder Taschke and Inditec with kind support of Okalux

IMAGES Katsuhisa Kida (Fototeca)

WORKSHOP MODELS Students of the Faculties for Architecture of FH Frankfurt, FH Wiesbaden, TU Darmstadt, RWTH Aachen instructed by Takaharu + Yui Tezuka (30 April – 7 May 2009); Assistance: Dominik Zausinger, Kai Kasugai

WORKSHOP VIDEO artsite.tv

BANNER, POSTER, INVITATION CARD Gardeners, Frankfurt

PUBLIC RELATIONS Paul Andreas, Stefanie Lampe

REGISTRAR Anke Gabriel

EXHIBITION SETUP Christian Walter, Detlef Wagner-Walter, Enrico Hirsekorn, Paolo Brunino, Joachim Müller-Rahn, Gerhard Winkler

ADMINISTRATION STAFF Inka Plechaty, Jeanette Bolz, Pascale Baier

KURATOR / KOORDINATION Paul Andreas

KONZEPT Peter Cachola Schmal, Takaharu + Yui Tezuka, Paul Andreas

AUSSTELLUNGSDESIGN Takaharu + Yui Tezuka, Kai Kasugai, Matthias Neuendorf, Midori Taki (Tezuka Architects)

UMSETZUNG Mario Lorenz (Deserve) mit Gebrüder Taschke und Inditec mit freundlicher Unterstützung von Okalux

FOTOS Katsuhisa Kida (Fototeca)

WORKSHOP-MODELLE Studierende der Fakultäten für Architektur der FH Frankfurt, FH Wiesbaden, TU Darmstadt und der RWTH Aachen unter Leitung von Takaharu + Yui Tezuka (30. April – 7. Mai 2009); Assistenz: Dominik Zausinger, Kai Kasugai

WORKSHOP VIDEO artsite.tv

BANNER, PLAKAT, EINLADUNGSKARTE Gardeners, Frankfurt

PRESSE- UND ÖFFENTLICHKEITSARBEIT Paul Andreas, Stefanie Lampe

REGISTRAR Anke Gabriel

AUSSTELLUNGSAUFBAU Christian Walter, Detlef Wagner-Walter, Enrico Hirsekorn, Paolo Brunino, Joachim Müller-Rahn, Gerhard Winkler

VERWALTUNG Inka Plechaty, Jeanette Bolz, Pascale Baier